THANK YOU

A Tribute To
CHRIS CORNELL

By The Friends and Fans of

Chris Cornell

© 2017 Each written piece, photograph and artwork is copyright of the respective creator

© 2017 This collection copyright of Angela J. Maher

Cover photo © 2015 Dawn Belotti

All rights reserved.

ISBN: 154815072X
ISBN-13: 978-1548150723

DEDICATION

For Chris Cornell.

A legend, always.

CONTENTS

    Introduction

1   Adam Baczkowski   1

2   Akef Haidar   2

3   Alexandra Sallan Lerena   5

4   Ali Khan   7

5   Alison Pereira   8

6   Allison Therese   9

7   Andrea Cook   10

8   Andrew Goldberg   11

9   Andy Hill   13

10   Angela J. Maher   14

11   Anita M.   17

12   Anne Knox   19

13   Annette McClellan   21

14   Arabella Cornell   24

15   Arletta Przynoga   25

16   Aynsley Dickinson   29

BY THE FANS AND FRIENDS OF CHRIS CORNELL

17	Bee Daly	30
18	Ben Stewart	31
19	Beth Guiles	32
20	Beth Langley	34
21	Billy Poulin	35
22	Bobby Buchholtz	36
23	Brian Kettler	37
24	Brian Martin	38
25	Brittany Peck	40
26	Brook Brown	42
27	Bryan Gibson	43
28	Camilla Troy	44
29	Caroline Morgan	45
30	Ceejay Alba	47
31	Charlotte Lee Demakos	48
32	Cheryl Farmer	50
33	ChrisCornellFanpage	51
34	Christina Baldonado	52
35	Christina Flores	54

36	Christine Layoff	55
37	Christy Pifer	56
38	Chylar	58
39	Cindy Mefford	60
40	Connie Law Lee	61
41	Craig Bradley	62
42	Cris Vedder	63
43	Crystal Ross	64
44	Csaba Mester	66
45	D.L.	68
46	Dani V. Brantley	69
47	Danielle Arthur	70
48	Darci Mabe	71
49	David E. Dickinson	74
50	Dawn Belotti	75
51	Dawn Carroll	79
52	de Vie weinstock	80
53	Deanna Lynn	84
54	Debbie Abrams Moore	86

55	Deborah Levesque	88
56	Desda Sayer	89
57	Desiree Jo Ruiz	90
58	Diane McDonald-Topping	92
59	Doc Thomas	94
60	Donna Barton	102
61	Dora Guadalupe Zalazar	103
62	Doug Daigle	104
63	Emilio Di Tullio	105
64	Emily Wagner	106
65	Eric Esrailian	123
66	Erin McElroy	124
67	Eva Puma	126
68	Fantastic Negrito	127
69	Gaby Nieva	130
70	Gaia Cornell	132
71	Galaxy Starr	134
72	Giles Kristian	136
73	Gina DiNolfi McMillen	137

74	Glad Ruiz	138
75	Greta Kennedy	139
76	Heather N.E. Jones	142
77	Holly Curtis	144
78	Ingrid Crane	145
79	Ivonne Caro	146
80	Jacqueline S.	148
81	Jade Bars	152
82	Jade Fish	153
83	Jamal Sampson	154
84	James Benger	155
85	James Howton	158
86	Janet Hall	160
87	Janine Munson	162
88	Jared Schmidt	164
89	Jason C. Geer	166
90	Jay Cee Lopez	168
91	Jeff Anderson	170
92	Jenifer Farmer	174

93	Jenni Hollister	175
94	Jennifer D. Burke	176
95	Jennifer Wallace	178
96	Jerry D. Traurig	179
97	Jill Haley	180
98	Joanne Roughsedge	181
99	Jodi Smith	183
100	Joe Broussard IV	184
101	John Barbara	186
102	John Eric Osborn	187
103	Joseph Baker	188
104	Jovelle Baker	191
105	Julie Harris	192
106	Julie McNamara	194
107	Julie Timmons	196
108	Julio Zaldivar Suarez	198
109	Justine Kores	201
110	Karen Verbeek	202
111	Karey Hanson-Brennan	204

112	Kari Reyes	207
113	Kasey Maynor	208
114	Kate Glencross	210
115	Kathy Nieboer	212
116	Katy Banteah	215
117	Kellen Morse	216
118	Kelly McFadyen	218
119	Kera Berutti	220
120	Kerrie Dixon	222
121	Kimberly Bennett	224
122	Kimmie Andersen	226
123	Kris Andrade	228
124	Krista Strogilis Bramon	230
125	Kristin Sanna Imperiale	233
126	L.S.	234
127	Laurie Rosso	235
128	Leo Petrovski	236
129	Leslie Cross	238
130	Lilly Dunne	240

131	Lily Rodriguez McLoughlin	242
132	Lisa Dalachinsky	243
133	Lisa McCaffrey	245
134	Lisa Moore Corley	246
135	Lisa Ryan	247
136	Lisa Vickers	248
137	Liz Eismendi	251
138	Lloyd Hendricks	252
139	Lois Giles	254
140	Lucas Santos	256
141	Lucy Clifton Sims	258
142	Lucy Hannaford	260
143	Lyn Shelle	262
144	Maggie Partridge	263
145	Mari Brown	264
146	Maricruz Rowley	265
147	Marisa Cassiano	267
148	Maureen Wells	268
149	Meg Kenning	269

150	Melina Pereira Vai	271
151	Melissa Christensen	274
152	Melissa Mazzoni Clark	277
153	Mia B. Becker	278
154	Michael J. Falotico	280
155	Michelle Deffinger	282
156	Michelle Evans and Diana Walker	284
157	Michelle Sharp	285
158	Mickey Horvath Gombosi	287
159	Mike Harrington	288
160	Miriam Maiorano	293
161	Monica M. Rosales	294
162	Myra Baucum	295
163	Nairi Sargsyan	296
164	Nancy Jane Bragg	299
165	Narene Russell	300
166	Nathan Wesley	302
167	Nathaniel Rawiri	304
168	Nicole Finch	305

169	Nina K.	306
170	Patty De Michele-Insigne	308
171	Paul Stensrud	309
172	Pete Thorn	310
173	Piera Alessio and Mary Chiodo Jennings	311
174	R. Scott Mattingly	316
175	Rachel Dunay Joseph	318
176	Rachelle Kanuch	319
177	Rebecca Meadows	320
178	Regina Keehfuss	321
179	Rhonda Bates	322
180	Rhonda Giannasi	323
181	Robert Brooks	324
182	Rochelle Weinard	326
183	Rocio Alvarez	327
184	Ron Cameron	331
185	Ron Hunt	332
186	Rory Jennings	337
187	Rose Hurt	338

188	Rose-Lea Otten-Sadowski	341
189	Ryan Gavalier	342
190	Sacha McGowan	344
191	Sam Harris	346
192	Samantha Lynn	347
193	Samarra Black	348
194	Samuel Fiunte Matarredona	355
195	Scott Browne	358
196	Scott Kvasni	359
197	Sean May	361
198	Shane McIntire	362
199	Shanida Carter	366
200	Sharon Edwards	368
201	Shubhang Joshi	370
202	Stephanie Gordon	371
203	Stephanie Mackley	373
204	Stephanie Munoz	374
205	Stephanie Silva	380
206	Stephen Coppola	381

207	Sue Ann VanGilder	383
208	Susan B. Harty	384
209	Sylvia Lee	385
210	Tamara Ann	386
211	Taryn Lee Thompson	387
212	Terri Parks	388
213	Tessa Jamerson	390
214	Tiffany Brook Meyer	394
215	Tiffany Van Drimlen	395
216	Tina Arvanites Dumont	396
217	Tina Brown	397
218	Tina Marie Chappell	399
219	Tom McMahon	400
220	Toni Harvey	401
221	Tony Hejnicki	403
222	Tuire Höynälä	404
223	Tyler Ruffle-McDonald	405
224	Uo Kaolly	410
225	Val J.	412

226	Vicky Appenzeller	413
227	Vincent Meeks	415
228	Wonder Sar	416
229	Yvonne Photias	417
230	Zacarius Hill	421
231	Zær Ben Abdallah	424
232	Final Words	426

Introduction

When news broke of the sudden death of rock music legend Chris Cornell fans were left in shock. Surely it was just another of those cruel celebrity death hoaxes? It couldn't be true! But as the news persisted and no denials came from official sources, it became apparent that it was real.

In the waves of shock and grief that followed, his fans from all around the globe began posting tributes, writing poems and blogs, and sharing memories. In these there were beauty and solace. A treasury of emotion and remembrance, but many of these posts were destined to drift away into cyberspace as time passed. Then, the idea for this book was born.

Within these pages you will find a collection of pieces written by his fans and his friends in the aftermath. Ranging from a few lines through to a number of pages, these paint a picture of the reaction to Chris Cornell's death. It's a picture of love and gratitude, as well as the expected deep grief.

This is a tribute, a love letter, and a legacy combined. Some pieces have been hand-picked from Facebook and Twitter posts, or blogs, many others were made as a direct submission.

All posts and images included in this book have been reprinted with permission from the original creators, and all rights are retained by them.

Adam Baczkowski

I'll never forget the time Chris Cornell so graciously invited me on stage to play "Spoonman" with him and the rest of the band. Devastated would be a huge understatement to describe my current mindset. Chris's music has gotten me through many rough periods in my life, as I'm sure the same could apply to many of you, and it's still been pretty tough to listen to his music these last two days without tearing up. I don't know when I'll start to feel more positive, but I'm sure that with such an amazing group of family [his fans], we can all get through this together. I miss ya, Chris.

Akef Haidar

Chris Cornell,

I've been watching how people react to what's happened. Grieving in different ways, but no one less than the next. People lamenting, truly, the loss of a friend, not just the devastating hole left in the music. There's a lot said about him. The voice, the songs, the good-hearted family man... the struggle to understand how this guy, this elected, eclectic prince, loved by all, really could come to that point.

The constant enigma of: Why did it happen? Why are we so personally devastated? It comes down to this... more than the musical talent. More than the voice. Every single person grieving feels like they knew Chris and that, in a way, that he knew them.

And even though you knew he was widely loved and immensely popular, it's almost weird to see grief the same as your own so widespread, because despite him connecting so deeply with millions, his music always felt like it was just you and him, handling the weight of life privately and personally. That's a rare thing, even amongst the greats.

My opinion? He was, until his death, the modern king of rock...

But more importantly, the thing I haven't heard said...

The king of catharsis.

His demons were secret to no one, nor were his kindness or his desire to be known as a full and rounded human being, not a rock caricature or a legend.

Chris... man... that guy could let go... he let it go on every song and every record... he let it go so masterfully that if you were nearby or heard a recording you let your weight go too. He unloaded your shit for you, just osmotically.

He guided you through it, by guiding himself through it. He let it go in every shade and color of the spectrum.

If you were broken and quiet and looking for the pieces of yourself, Chris had let that go on a song somewhere and could help you through it.

If you were in a fit of manic rage, Chris had let that go in a song somewhere and could help you through it.

Ask ten fans what their favorite records are and you'll get ten different answers.

Tributes to him range from Norah Jones to Megadeth, Cat Stevens to Incubus. Prolific. Period. That's the bar for that term. Chris Cornell set it, and probably didn't even care whether he did or not.

Then we got to watch him survive the grunge heyday, beat his addiction, lose his voice, get it back, get centered, become, seemingly, happy, come back stronger than ever.

We looked at this guy like, the demons he beat.... that's hope. That's inspiration. Maybe, I'll be okay.

He was, by virtue of being himself, our medicine man. Watching him end this way is so hard.

He was such a role model in so many ways, and I always thought, but yeah "He's also just a good dude who kept pushing through."

I realize now that I was kidding myself... he was more than human to me, like so many others. It's easy to see why, but it wasn't fair to him.

If his family and bandmates should ever read this: Chris Cornell, and, I think he'd want me to acknowledge that Matt, Kim and Ben also, saved my life over and over again, and I am far from alone.

Thank you all for taking care of him. I can't say or do anything that'll make it better, but his impact is beyond words or even comprehension. In grief, it's easy to lose sight of.

I think I speak for legions when I say, we are thankful to have lives that coincided with his.

We're here for you.

Thank you, Chris Cornell.

Alexandra Sallan Lerena

My life changed the day I found a magazine in a music store in Barcelona. It was NME, and on the cover was a picture of a film. A film about four young Seattle friends. Probably because at that time I knew that Nirvana were from that city I got obsessed with the magazine. Next to the article were some photos of the movie, and one of the pictures called my attention. One with the director of the film with three guys called, Eddie, Layne and Chris. I felt in love immediately. The article mentioned the soundtrack, and that happened to be my new objective, to convince my mother to buy it for me, and when finally I got it, GOD! I found my new life.

From that moment, I did not care about not having friends, or not having anyone to hangout. I just wanted to save money during the week so I could buy a record on Friday, lock myself in my room for two days and devour the CDs from top to bottom.

First I got *Ultramega OK*, later *Louder Than Love*, *Badmotorfinger*. In between I found Temple Of The Dog (and Pearl Jam, Alice In Chains). Those records made me felt that I was not alone. That there was someone who understood my despair at not knowing how to fit into society. And the best thing, they were still recording albums and doing tours.

In 1994 *Superunknown* came out, and if the other records had lit the wick, this one caused the explosion. My parents were against my music obsession; they did not understand it, and they did not let me got to the Soundgarden concert on 21st September, 1996 at the Pabelló Oímpic de Vall d´Hebrón in Barcelona. I wanted to die. Neither the cries nor the tears worked. Nothing made them change their opinion. It was horrible but on 25th October, 1999 everything changed, because then I was able to attend the concert that he gave in my city with the *Euphoria Morning* tour.

It was wonderful. He took the stage a little bit drunk but what a show! Amazing. I left the venue with the feeling that everything was possible. Maximum happiness. Life was good. The same day of that show I saw him walking along the ramblas, in Barcelona. He seemed calm and adorable. I looked at him and thought, oh my god! It's Chris Cornell!,.. but I could not say anything. He passed by my side and, that's it. I stood there looking at him and thinking what a great opportunity I had just lost.

He returned one year ago but, because of damn money, I could not afford the ticket, and to comfort myself I thought, ok!... you will see him next time, he will come back.

And now he is gone. I will never have the chance to look at him in the eyes and say, "Thank you. Thank you for probably giving me the best youth that nobody has ever had. Thank you for being there when no one else was. Thank you for your friendship."

They say we have to try to get the positive side of bad things. From Chris' death, I've learnt, if you can do it, if you want to do it, then DO IT! because life may not give you this chance again.

Ali Khan

Goodbye, celestial being. Forever my Rock God, forever my all. I love you. Always will. You're my everything. Thank you for everything.

Alison Pereira

Chris, your voice has been the soundtrack of my life and has helped me through some of the darkest moments of depression. Today my heart is heavy. I hear your voice in my head everyday but it's my heart you will forever resonate within. Our searchlight soul. Thank you for always being there for me and for reminding me I am not alone.

Alison Pereira - Vancouver, BC.

Allison Therese

Dear Chris, I have tried many times to put into writing what is in my heart, but I still cannot express it. Simply put, you have held a special place in my heart for years, and you always will. A piece of me is lost without you in this world. Your passing is tragic on many levels. Thank you for the songs you have given to us.

Andrea Cook

Your words give me strength. Your voice gives me joy. Your music has shaped my life. You have been the one constant, and for that I thank you.

Andrew Goldberg

To the rest of Soundgarden fans and family, this is from August 14th 2014 in Tampa, Florida.

This was my first ever concert since originally having my two major open heart surgeries, all artificial heart valves, dialysis and a pacemaker. It was the Dillinger Escape Plan, Soundgarden and Nine Inch Nails. All my doctors, myself, and everyone thought I'd never live to see this concert but God had other plans and I did see it, thankfully.

Anyway, much of the beginning of the day was horrible and dreadful awful. It was constantly storming, pretty awfully on and off all day and it was outside at the Tampa Amphitheatre. We had second thoughts about actually going because of horrible weather, etc, the whole trip there but we continued to push forward.

We got there it was cold and wet and windy. During the The Dillinger Escape Plan opening act it wouldn't stop pouring at all. Then, the news came in that actor comedian Robin Williams had committed suicide by hanging. Everybody there was shocked and devastated by the news. Just as this was happening, Soundgarden was taking the stage. Then, something that I will never forget happened.

It still feels like it was just yesterday, as a matter of fact.

Until recently, I never put much thought into it or really understood what was going on at that moment in time. Soundgarden started playing the song "Searching With My Good Eye Closed", and I will never forget during the song all of a sudden it stopped pouring rain and the clouds parted. The sky opened up and it was like heaven itself opened up and these bright beams of golden sunlight were hitting the audience, the stage, and Chris Cornell as well. Chris Cornell took notice and his voice was so powerful and commanding when he kept looking up to the heavens and singing the lyrics "Is it to the sky?" over and over. It was as if he was signing to God Personally Himself. It was such an emotional and intense moment in time that I'll never forget as long as I'm alive. I hope you enjoyed my personal story of Chris Cornell.

Andy Hill

I had the privilege to see CC perform seven times. The last was his acoustic solo set at Benaroya Hall in Seattle in October 2013. I was third row back front-and-center, thanks to some jackass next to my ticketed seat up/back in mezzanine, who was drunk during the opening act, making harassing comments to me. I complained to event staff, and they relocated me to an available seat in the third row front and center!!

The show was unlike any other concert. An intimate fireside where he was kicking back with all the fans.

Anyone who has been in Benaroya Hall knows about its acoustic design. When it's quiet, you can hear a pin drop (it was designed for the Seattle symphony). At the show, CC said "this place feels too sacred to play rock", then yells "Fuck! There, now its been sullied and is ready".

Best memory from the show: During one of those periods of sheer silence between songs, someone from the crowd (wish it was me) yells out: "Chris ... Fucking ... Cornell". Everyone heard it. Perfectly spoken, perfectly timed. Three simple words to define his legendary status. Everyone cheered and screamed. Chris cracked a smile.

Angela J. Maher

Chris meant more to me than even I realised, which is saying something...

I fell in love with his voice long before I knew his name or even what he really looked like. Then, somewhere along the way, he captured my heart. He became even more after tweeting a picture of a marble wall and asking what could we see? I saw a scene, then a paragraph, then a chapter... In that moment he became my muse. It wasn't by choice (although who better could I have chosen?). After that everything I wrote had at least a taste of his influence. I wish that he had known that. I wish he'd known his interviews encouraged me as much as his songs gave me solace. I love him with a purity few people ever receive from me.

My beautiful muse, you have broken my heart. But I gladly feel this pain in payment for the miracle of you having existed at all.

Rest peacefully.

THANK YOU: A TRIBUTE TO CHRIS CORNELL

BY THE FANS AND FRIENDS OF CHRIS CORNELL

@AngelaJMaher The song Higher Truth was. What's on the record is the original version but I wrote about 5 different ones.

Anita M.

Dear Chris,

This is too surreal! Why? Why are you gone? Why am I grieving so immensely for you? We aren't family, we're not friends, we're not even acquaintances. Is it because depression consumes me too to the point of having dark thoughts almost everyday? Is it because I feel like an outcast, a loner and a loser? Or is it because the very first time I heard your songs from *Superunknown* ("Black Hole Sun", "The Day I Tried To Live", "Fell On Black Days") that helped me feel I wasn't alone in my struggles?

I made mix tapes with these very songs back in 1994/1995 and your voice and lyrics still resonate in my life. Maybe this is why I'm grieving for you. I really wanted to go to your last concert at the Fox Theater on May 17th. It wasn't too far away! I regret not going! :(

So many emotions are flowing through me; shock, sorrow, anger, sadness to name a few. This is where your songs help ease the pain. Unfortunately you are no longer here to sing them in person.

But all I can do right now is give much love to you and

your family. This sounds so cheesy but you will truly be missed and be in my completely broken heart. Your words will continue to uplift everyone in fact.

Photo: Pixabay

Anne Knox

Music is my therapy since age five when I got my first radio. The first time I saw Soundgarden I believe it was 1990, but not sure. They opened for Faith No More at the Trocadero in Philly. I was there to see SG.

I have seen SG and CC solo to many times to count. I wish I could remember all the shows. My late husband had the awesome memory. He passed on 22nd April, 2014 from suicide. So to say the least, I feel the same right now as I did when my husband passed.

Over the years I have been lucky enough to see SG and collect some things along the way. I now cherish my setlists, picks, autographs, etc, even more than I did before. A few years back I was looking at chriscornell.com and clicked on one of the *Songbook* shows I saw in November 2011 in Atlantic City. I was ecstatic when I saw the pictures of Chris Cornell shaking my hand on Chris's website. I messaged the photographer asking for a copy but never heard back from her.

One time I packed a backpack, tickets in hand, and hopped on the Megabus to see Chris Cornell at the Bowery Ballroom (that is where I got my blue CC pick) and the next night was Irving Plaza. What amazing shows and so much fun waiting in line with fellow Knights. When we went to Hammerstein show in NYC, it was freezing. We brought cardboard to sit on, someone brought a kerosene heater that helped. My late husband was offered clothes from people walking by, they thought we were homeless, but no, just waiting to get on the rail for that show. I got some really amazing pictures there. One of my favorites is Chris's reflection in Matt's drum.

Another awesome memory from NYC. Was waiting for Ben to come out of the venue. Everyone else from the band already left, so being me I walked over to his esclade and started talking to his driver asking when he was coming out. During that time someone came out and asked the driver to drive around the block so they could get a truck up the street. I asked the driver if I could come for the ride He said yes, so I got to sit in Ben's seat and take a ride. I should have written him a note as I always have a sharpie with me at all concerts I ever go to, and I go to a lot of concerts.

I could probably write a book, there are so many more shows I could write about but I don't want to make this too long. I have always loved TOTD was accepting the fact I would never see that show. Well TOTD decided to tour and they were coming to my hometown Upper Darby PA to the Tower Theater, one of my all time favorite venues. I knew it was going to be impossible to get tickets, I was so nervous. The first show was on my late husband's birthday so I guess his energy left on earth helped me get my 13th row tickets. But at the Tower I always end up 3rd row right side been the same security guard for years there. When I got to the Tower that night I immediately went to the box office and asked if they had tickets for tomorrow night and they did 5th row on left side. I couldn't believe it. Dreams do come true. Never thought I would ever see TOTD. That was the last night I saw Chris Cornell.

Annette McClellan

Chris Cornell, My mom, and Me

This is about my first time to see Chris Cornell live.

His music helped me through a very dark place in my life during late 2015-early 2016. In late February my mom was taken to the ER with what was thought to be another cardiac event. She never recovered.

During those two weeks, Chris announced he'd be playing at Ravinia near Chicago. Mom was teaching me from her hospital bed that life was too short, to go for what I wanted to do. So I told my father that if I had to sleep in my car and eat peanut butter crackers to see him, I was going to.... harrumph!

My mom passed March 5. On March 6 (also my dad's birthday), Chris announced the entire North American tour. There were three places all within a reasonable distance. I decided I would go for one of those.

March 7 (also the anniversary of my mom's mom's passing; freaky, no?) I'm sitting in the mortuary helping finalize Mom's arrangements. My Ticketmaster app buzzed and only one of my locations was operating through them. I couldn't stop to call the nearest venue, but I could do this one (next closest). So I got my ticket - don't laugh, the mortician was running late.

I got home later and looked up the seat on the venue's website - my mother and grandmother gave me one of the most precious gifts ever. My seat was 5th row, almost exact center stage (#20 on a row of 38). I cried buckets. I could not believe it. It was my first ever Chris Cornell show in any version. It was going to be magical.

And it was.

And Mom continued to work her magic - I got tickets to Temple in NYC; a friend ended up with a spare for Seattle and asked me to join her. I got tickets for Carolina Rebellion and then with days to spare, lucky enough for an opportunity to see them the next night in Tuscaloosa.

This morning in the grey dreary rain, on the way to church, I had a heart-to-heart crying conversation with my mother. I thanked her for all she'd done to help me see my favorite artist so many times in such a short time frame. I also told her to please find him in heaven and to give him a huge hug and thank him for meaning so much to me and countless others. I asked her to keep his sweet family and close friends in her prayers as well.

I don't always subscribe to a traditional understanding of theology. I honestly don't know what the afterlife holds... my own thought is that we're bathed in light and goodness and that love fills every missing piece, all the gaps. And so I pray and hope with all my being that whatever gaps were there have been filled to overflowing with light and love... and that the overspill comes down and makes us better people for it.

Loud love my friends.

Photo: Dawn Belotti

With Soundgarden, Hammerstein, January 22, 2013.

Arabella Cornell

I'm still reeling from the loss of Chris Cornell. An awesome voice and handsome face were just the tip of the iceberg. He was a musical genius, an inspiration, a muse to many, and the kindest of hearts. Although I never met him, I will remember him forever, with love.

Arletta Przynoga

I actually started listening to Chris Cornell from the *Scream* album. It was summer and I had to go to hospital, to the dermatological department for two weeks. I was staying in a room with five more ladies: one with serious case of cancer, on top of that with nasty dermatological problems on her face, one which was obese and it caused troubles with her health (and she made so much noise at nights) and a little girl - maybe 10 years old, totally scared.

The nights were really tough in this room, with painful moaning, snoring, crying of the people. The second day a friend brought me *Scream* on CD. And I started to listen to it 24/7. Day and night, especially nights. It really helped me. Then I got *Euphoria Morning* and *Carry On*, and then Audioslave, and then Soundgarden albums - so I went sort of backward.

After leaving the hospital, I started following Chris Cornell and found out that he was very active on Twitter. I didn't believe my English was good enough (it was really bad at that time). But I figured, I can sign in to Twitter and just follow him. And then I started tweeting a little. And that's how I met some of the most wonderful people: Rose, Sabrina, Marlen, Trudy, Shelli, Sarah, Dianne, Mayra, Fabiola, Jo ... and many,

BY THE FANS AND FRIENDS OF CHRIS CORNELL

Photo: Piera Alessio

many more. His amazing, open family (I so cherish the message from Mrs. Toni Karayiannis when I sent her a photo from my University graduation and she wrote back "we are all proud of you").

I really made friendships (even if only online, they are real). I got strength from Chris Cornell's music and support from the community of people surrounding him, in the time of doubts, in the time of hurting myself and going through my own black days. His music, the lyrics, they were (still are) a vent to let out the bad emotions. They are my musical blocker of demons. Now, writing these words, I feel incredibly selfish and awful that I had that vent in his music, but he seemed to miss his own Chris Cornell vent...

I am beyond grateful that a friend of mine from a local University radio station where I worked took me to Soundgarden concert at Zitadelle Spandau in Berlin for my first SG concert. When they played "Drawing Flies" I cried. When they ended with "Beyond The Wheel" I couldn't catch my breath. Then another friend gave me a ticket to see them again in Berlin at Columbia Halle. I stood in the second row the whole show and was in heaven. The last - and most special concert of Soundgarden to me - was the one and only Polish show. In 2014, at Live Festival Oświęcim. The amazing Polish girls – Kasia and Ismeril - brought a huge Polish flag which we could sign. They were in the first row and threw it to the band. Chris took it and there is a photo of him holding it still after the show. That was as close as I got to Mr. Chris Cornell. My biggest dream was to see his solo show. I didn't make it. But I am beyond grateful for the three chances to see Soundgarden which I got.

In the meantime, a group of us - CC friends from Twitter - came up with a birthday gift for his 50th birthday. We got a t-shirt, which we all wanted to sign and in the end figure out a way to deliver to him. It went to Argentina, Honduras, USA, Poland, we signed for a friend in Canada... we got stuck in Italy and have Germany and Netherlands still on our list. Yes, we didn't finish on time. Any time. But it connected us so much.

The magic of his music and his personality.

Getting introduced to Chris Cornell's music changed so much in my life. I got the courage and self-acceptance that I never thought I would be capable of having. Two years ago I got the best gift ever on my birthday - he followed me on Twitter. Small thing, but when you sit on a 12 hours night shift in a crappy hotel and think there is nothing good coming in your life, such thing can really change a lot. I quit that job, got a really good and interesting one, and really thought that things can happen, if you work for them.

In between of all that I mentioned above, I kept on coming back to "I am the Highway" - which became my anthem, soundtrack of my life.

As tears can't stop running on my face since yesterday, I am also so happy that I didn't miss his music, his existence and was able to follow it in a company of wonderful people. I believe we will still follow the music together and that is the most comforting thought right now. You will all stay in my life, as he will stay in our hearts and thoughts.

I send one more big virtual hug to everyone who got touched by this death and are trying to cope with it and to say their own goodbye.

Aynsley Dickinson

It's not like I've lost a family member... It's deeper than that. I've lost part of my musical DNA. Which to me means part of my soul has died. As dramatic as that sounds – it's true. Most of the bands I've been in have a debt to Chris. I'm a drummer and subconsciously I've been taking lessons from Matt Cameron... But in turn I think he's been inspired to play like he does in Soundgarden from Chris. It all ties together. My singer in the band I'm in is influenced by Chris (in reviews he gets compared to Chris, oddly - I don't see it personally but hey....) And Layne... It's just that Chris has influenced everyone in the last 30 years whether we consciously know it or not. This hurts. This really fucking HURTS.
My heart aches.

Bee Daly

Thanks for the inspiration - Zurich, 1999.

Ben Stewart

I'll never forget seeing them for the first time when I was 16 in Sydney way back in 1994. Whoa, so awesome I was amazed. Was always a massive fan since then. A friend and I went to check them out last time they came to Sydney. Wow, they still had it. What a great night. Have loved all your music, Chris. Grew up with it. I've been pumping the Soundgarden lately. Oh man, what a voice. You will be sorely missed. By your family, your friends and your fans. RIP Chris Cornell.

Beth Guiles

My Friend
Your blue eyes held the truth
There'll never be another you,
I wish I could have known
That you felt so alone.
Why did you leave this way?
There are not words to say
Just what you meant to me
Now it will never be.
Beauty in your words
Carried on wings of gold
You lifted me with those wings
And all the joy untold.
Tears stream down my face
For you have gone away
A hole in my heart
My world torn apart.
But I will carry on
Your song in my heart
And take what you gave to me
And we will never part…

Copyright 2017 singr1964

THANK YOU: A TRIBUTE TO CHRIS CORNELL

Journey

On my journey I ran into you
Voice like diamonds, eyes of blue
Thought the times were gonna last
Never thought it'd turn into the past.
Rivers run within the golden sun
Music filled the ears of everyone
Never thought the music would end
Never thought I would lose my friend
Gone, you are gone like the wind
But your song remains in my heart,
Gone, into the
Arms of Love
In His house you will not part.
Sing, the song is on my lips
Fill the world with songs of love.
Sing, and carry on
Sing, and carry on
In His house the music never ends.

Copyright 2017 singr1964

Beth Langley

Thank you for the music, Chris. You will never be forgotten.

Billy Poulin

Hi. I would like to say a prayer for our brother.

Dear Chris, I pray for you continually, that you have found peace and everlasting life. All souls are part of God who is the God of LIFE so you will always be a part of LIFE Chris. Your music and voice and charisma were the most creative and talented the world has ever had and it lives on. You've inspired my own music and poetry. Thank you, Chris.

What it really feels like is a part of us has died. The music of Chris and Soundgarden, as well as Temple Of The Dog and Audioslave, reached to the very depths of our souls and especially Chris's singing. That has been ripped from our lives and it hurts us bad. RIP Chris you are severely missed.

Bobby Buchholtz

I have been mezmerized by the unique style that is Soundgarden from the beginning. Chris is the warrior poet, in my opinion, and I was discouraged through the years that more people could not grasp the beauty and the message.
I am glad to be in such humbling company today with the outpouring of emotions and genuine love for the band and extreme sadness and confusion at news of Chris's passing. I have been a musician all my life, but did not take up singing seriously until I was inspired by Chris. I wanted to sing with that level of emotion and actually say something meaningful.

Never have words echoed so loudly in my headspace. I miss you.

Brian Kettler

I know we all know how amazing, transcendent, and genre-busting Chris's voice is but what about the lyrics? If I ever got the chance to meet him I would've told him to me he was my generation's Bob Dylan lyrically. He has inspired me so much as a writer I wouldn't even know where to start. I guess for me it was when I heard the lyrics to "Mind Riot". But especially the first time my ears were lucky enough to hear one particular line in "Rusty Cage". Damn. Mind = blown. Gone were simplistic and generic hair metal lyrics. This was Kerouac.

Brian Martin

I wrote this about Chris Cornell. It's called *Help Me*. It's like me saying how important he was to me, and Chris telling me it's alright just keep playing his songs.

Help Me

You have been in my life
My therapy
The words of your wisdom
Echoed in my soul
Now that you're gone
I still don't have to let you go
Help me make it through
Help me live without you
Help me breathe the life you shared
For the love of music that you cared
Help me
Help me
I have no rage
That you are gone

THANK YOU: A TRIBUTE TO CHRIS CORNELL

Like many years before
To me you will be here for good
Pray for me
Come back again
To me you could
Of walked on water
Pray for me
Come back again
Help me
Help live in peace
Look up to the stars
I'm far away
But I'll come back again
In your heart
With every song
WITH EVERY SONG
You will get a part of me
I will come back again
With every song
Help me rest in peace
With every song
Don't turn it off
DON'T TURN IT OFF

Brittany Peck

Picture it... NY, 1996. I'm 10 years old. I'm in my room crying, after my mom once again dragged me to my room by my hair. I don't remember what I did this time. And the entire way to my room she's saying: "don't you cry, you little bitch". I blast Soundgarden and scream along to the lyrics in "My Wave". Then I switch to "Head Down", and I feel like Chris is there holding my hand. Telling me he sees me. I wasn't alone.

2003. I'm 16 now and got into self injury and have suicidal thoughts. I listen to "Blow Up The Outside World". I'm again not alone. I feel like Chris knows what I'm going through. He's been there. Chris was my voice.

2010, first introduction for my daughter. I play the *Superunknown* album over and over until my three-year-old knows all the words.

2017, my world crumbles. March 1st was four years since my amazing friend passed away, and every year gets harder. March 20th my best friend's fiancé passes away. A person I've known since she was born. I watch her heart break in front of my eyes. 24th - my client passes away the day she told me I was like another daughter to her. All I have is Chris's words. April 7th, I'm going for an operation I've had before but going under is hard for me with my high anxiety. I listen to SG as I go under. May 18th I wake up to the worst news. My knight has died.

My voice is gone. I cry for days. I can't listen to his music. Then I listened to "Black Hole Sun" when it came on the radio. My daughter runs out and starts singing and hugs me and says: "Mom, he's in our hearts forever". Held me so tight.

June 15th my daughter and I start our 23 push ups for 23 days.

Chris was my voice when I was voiceless, my light when I was dark. My world is now a bit darker. Things don't look as bright. My life will never be the same. Thank you, Chris, for all you did for me and the world. You live on in me and my daughter. "When the people we love are stolen from us, the way to have them live on is to never stop loving them."

Brook Brown

Saw you in Montreal for the *Euphoria Morning* tour. I was front row and you held my hand when you hit that high note on "Fell On Black Days". I shook all over. Almost twenty years later and I can still feel it. Thank you Chris for your music and making this planet a much better place. It won't be the same without you.

Bryan Gibson

Farewell, my friend. Your legacy will continue to shine throughout the universe. Today, tomorrow, forever. Thank you again, for everything.

Photo: Doc Thomas

Camilla Troy

Dear Chris,

I feel blessed for having chance to see you at your solo concerts. I completely fell in love with your voice, with your music. With the lyrics and the way you sing them. The concert in Vienna 2016 was a magical night with very spiritual moments.

I never met you in person but I always felt like you are the guy next door. Unbelievably humble, no poses of rock star. Funny guy who smiles most of the time. Very beautiful person, outside and inside. Spiritual. And the tenderness in your eyes always caresses my soul.

When it happened I realized that I am not living my life the way I wish. Today we are here thinking too much, waiting for something and tomorrow all is gone... I do not want to miss anything in my life. I do not want to blame myself for losing the moment to express my sympathy, my apology, my love.

We should do what makes us happy and we feel that it is right. We should spread the love and peace!

Chris, I love you... I miss you... forever! Thank you for helping to all of us in hard times. My heart is broken. Hope to meet you one day, angel. Loud love!

Caroline Morgan

Chris Cornell changed my life, as he changed the world. He let us all know we were not alone. We weren't weirdos, someone understood us. I know he understood me, my heart, my mind and he knew me so well that it made me see that I was really ok. He saw the darkness that I felt and he was ok, so I would be ok too. He was the poet of my generation, as well as the voice and the face. But he was also my friend and companion. Everyday he gave me hope and strength with every word he sang.

Chris' music has and will always be the soundtrack of my life. I only saw Soundgarden once but I will never forget it. It was in Memphis, 1992, with Guns N' Roses.

I was at Rocklahoma 2017. It should have been the final show of the tour. The Oklahoma sky cried with the world for him that night, closing down the stages and no one played. Only seemed appropriate that if Soundgarden couldn't play, no one else would either.

There will never be a day my heart doesn't hurt for him, his beautiful children, his family and band families. I will thank God everyday for giving him to us all, if only for a little while. Chris Cornell will live on till the end of time and inspire millions. I will continue to share him with as many souls as

possible.
Caroline Morgan
Stuttgart, Arkansas.

Photo: Pixabay

Ceejay Alba

Thank you for changing the course of music forever and giving joy to people's lives everywhere, including me and my Father – Bino.

Charlotte Lee Demakos

I can't even begin to listen or hear CC's voice right now. Swells of pain overflow into tears that have no control. Depending on the moment, I go through a myriad of emotions eventually ending in devastated sorrow. Sorrow for him, his family, friends, colleagues and yes, definitely for myself.

   Am I selfish? Sometimes I feel that way when I'm angry, as if I should have known. I'm lost with the knowledge that I no longer have his words, wisdom, music and life to follow throughout my years. It's been 30 years and I feel like I've lost my best friend, brother and therapist all in one. It'll be a long day coming for my heart to smile again. Hopefully, when it does - it will be for the years of joy he has given me and my husband, George Demakos, and will continue to do so with a legacy that makes legends legendary.

Photo: Dawn Belotti.

With Soundgarden, at Webster Hall. June 2, 2014.

Cheryl Farmer

You changed the Universe with your music Chris. Your gift as a poet and songwriter has made this a better place! And that voice. My God, that voice. All I can say is thank you for sharing these gifts with the world.

As much as it hurts and shocks, I pray for your family because I know their sorrow. But I know you are not really gone. We are all connected. You have changed worlds but are still a part of us all. You were a beautiful Angel here, and the burden you carried can be heard in the warmth and wisdom of your voice and your words. I'm truly sorry for that part! We do not judge! We will always love you. AHO Chris Cornell!

With deep respect I honor your memory.
Cheryl.

ChrisCornellFanpage

Your music was my safe place, your voice and words were my daily escape from this world. Now I can't listen to your songs anymore without tears in my eyes and pain in my chest. I feel lost and lonely, more than ever. I can't explain why it hurts so much.

    I feel like I'm being selfish and childish because, despite all the fucked up things happening in this world, I keep thinking about a person I'll never know. I can't help wondering why you.

Christina Baldonado

The Blackest Day

I woke up to almost the worst news I could ever hear,
My most favorite musician was no longer here.
I felt like I had been kicked right in the gut,
I couldn't breathe, or think, or speak, wait, what?
No! This can't be happening, it must be fake news.
That was just the beginning of my blackest day blues.
The tears started flowing and I just wanted to stay in bed,
But I had another very important matter to attend,
My own little dandelion, Delilah, was lying next to me.
I tried to compose myself and dry my eyes so she wouldn't see.
But I couldn't keep it together, my world was crashing down,
In the waves of sorrow washing over me, I was afraid I might drown.
I didn't want to believe that my Chris was no more,
Such an abrupt and unexpected slamming of life's door.
How could it be that this nightmare is true?
I will forever wonder what went wrong, were there clues?
I'll always love the way his dark curls sometimes covered his face
And how at other times he shook it all over the place.
To see him smile from across the stage, that alone could stop my heart,

THANK YOU: A TRIBUTE TO CHRIS CORNELL

Just one more beautiful thing that set him apart.
The bitter blue sparkle of his eyes now in eternal sleep
Are wide awake in the memories I will forever keep.
The voice that soothed my soul with his eloquent play with words
Would not ever sing to me the way it did before.
I feel like I lost my best friend even though I didn't know him at all
Because he was always with me through good and bad times, big things and small.
The worst part of all of this is not knowing why
In that very moment, he chose to say goodbye.
My heart hurts for his family, friends, and fans
As I try to make sense of this and make my plans.
I'll try to find my way the best way I know how,
And I guess there's nothing left to say but goodbye, for now.

Chris, I hope you found that better place you were looking for. I love you.

Christina Flores

Chris Cornell has been my favorite singer since I was 12 years old. His music means the world to me, it was my bible before I found Christ, and it was the first thing I turned to in happy or sad times. His songs helped me get through the most difficult times in my life, and were with me in the happiest times as well. They were the first and last songs that my husband Micah and I danced to at our wedding. Somehow I was able to wrangle Micah into my love for his music, and it made it that much more amazing to have someone else to share it with.

I was lucky enough to see him sing live eleven times, and I am really so sad that I won't get that chance again. I'm so thankful that he shared his music with the world, and I feel so blessed that I have all these amazing memories of his music and how happy it has made me and my life.

Christine Layoff

Christy Pifer

Thank you for 30 years of kick-ass music to workout to, clean the house to, ponder life to and take a long fast drive to! Thank you and I look forward to hearing your new music in the next life.

THANK YOU: A TRIBUTE TO CHRIS CORNELL

Photo: Yvonne Photias

Chylar

I met Chris Cornell backstage at a Soundgarden concert in New York, January 2013. I was thrilled to show him the portrait tattoo I had inked by Steve Tefft (Ink Master winner, Season 2). As I revealed the tattoo to Chris, he immediately replied, "I've always hated that picture of me."

THANK YOU: A TRIBUTE TO CHRIS CORNELL

Cindy Mefford

My husband has always been a solid Soundgarden fan. You get in his car, at any time, it's what's playing. Go to the basement and SG is either playing or he's trying to perfect the guitar portion of "Incessant Mace". I'm more into the solo work but he's full on Kevin's mom about his SG. The mutual love of The Doors is what brought us together as friends.

Back in the mid 90s, when we were just friends, we attended a festival show. I had gone to get a beverage and SG began to play as the sun set. I was so awestruck by hearing them cover "Waiting For The Sun" that I stood motionless. Moments later, the sea of 50,000 people parted and there stood my future husband. It was movie-like and one of the best moments of my life.

We are both deeply saddened by this loss. We've never grieved so hard for someone we didn't personally know. We had just seen him a week before his passing. Somehow that, combined with how etched he was in our daily lives through music, made it more personal.

We cherish our memories and are grateful, like you, to say we lived in the time of Chris Cornell.

~Russ & Cindy Mefford

Connie Law Lee

I was going through a lot bad times and Chris kept me going, through my bad marriage and helping me with my friend dying on me. He gave me hope and strength to go on and for him I will go on again.

Craig Bradley

Never in my life has a death in the music world shook me this way before. Kurt Cobain, Lynn Strait (Snot), Layne Staley, Ronnie James Dio, Peter Steele, Scott Weiland, Lemmy, just to name a few, and I'm a big fan of all of them. Well maybe not Nirvana, but I understand their importance in music history.

When I woke up for work Wednesday morning and found out that one of my rock heroes was gone, I immediately became washed over with feelings of disbelief and a sadness so great that I could literally feel my heart breaking. It's been three days and those same feelings are still with me. Since that fateful day, I've listened to nothing but his music. Depending on my mood would determine what album I put on.

As extensive as his catalog is, I find myself going back to three albums. *Badmotorfinger*, *Temple of the Dog*, and *Unplugged in Sweden*. Those three records have helped me through some of the toughest times in my life, and now they're going to help me get through this devastating loss.

Chris Cornell was a once in a lifetime artist, and I was lucky enough to see Soundgarden and Audioslave more than once. Of all the artists I mentioned earlier, this one is going to sting the worst for a long, long time.

Cris Vedder

Só tenho a agradecer ao Chris Cornell por ter me apresentado três bandas maravilhosas nos anos 90s: Temple Of The Dog, Soundgarden e Pearl Jam. Sua voz ecoa em meus ouvidos desde da primeira vez que ouvi e sua imagem não saiu mais da minha cabeca e coração. E anos mais tardes fez parte de outra banda que amo Audioslave. Obrigada Chris por td isso,suas músicas fazem parte da minha vida e vc sempre vivera em meu coração. Love from Brazil.

Interpretation:
I can only thank to Chris Cornell for having introduced myself three amazing bands in the 90s: Temple Of The Dog, Soundgarden, and Pearl Jam. Your voice echoes in my ears since the first time I heard his image and never came out of my head and heart. And years later was part of another band I love, Audioslave. Thank you Chris for all of this, their songs are part of my life and you always lived in my heart. Love, from Brazil.

Crystal Ross

I have been pretty quiet since I learned of Chris Cornell's death yesterday. Mostly because I am not sure how to put my feelings into words, and this will probably be a bit of rambling, and because I have been trying to process my grief as well. I am sure some people will scoff and say "he was just a celebrity", "he was just another famous person that committed suicide", or "we have more important people to focus on." But, if you truly know me and care about me, you will understand why this is so devastating for me, and why he is not just another celebrity to me. He was my number one, my absolute favorite musician. Soundgarden and Audioslave, no one can top them because of him.

When "Black Hole Sun" was released in 1994, I was 16 years old. My childhood was not an easy one, and my teenage years were filled with trauma and abuse. I had two things that I turned to as an escape: my horses and my music. Music is something that I have always connected with on a deeper level than most people. I don't just listen to music, I feel the music and the lyrics and the emotion in a singer's voice. When I first heard Chris Cornell's voice, there was an automatic connection, an attraction to the sound of his voice, I had to hear more and know more about him. And, on top of having an amazing voice, he was gorgeous.

He had a four octave vocal range, and man I felt every octave. He was so passionate in every note, the ways he could change the tone, the pitch of his voice gave me goosebumps, and still does. You could tell he was truly connected with his music. In my opinion, he has the best rock voice ever, bar none, and he was an amazing and gifted artist.

I have never met Chris, but I was so fortunate to see Soundgarden in concert twice. My very first concert, when I turned 18, was Soundgarden. They played at the Salem Armory and it kicked ass, totally set the bar for all of the 50+ concerts I have been to since. I also saw them in Portland about four years ago and he was amazing. To hear him sing live is truly an amazing gift, it is something that I will treasure for the rest of my life.

Even though I never had the chance to meet him, I have always felt a deep, personal connection to him. As silly as that might sound, his music, his words, his presence made my life better. His music (among others) is what kept me going in times of fear, sadness and uncertainty. I will mourn his death until mine, and maybe someday in the very, very distant future, I will get to thank him for the last 22 years of happiness that he and his music provided me. Until then, his music will live on through me, and the millions of other people who loved him. I truly hope he is now at peace, and I hope his family can find some peace too.

"Say Hello to Heaven..."

Crystal Ross. Dallas, Oregon USA.

Csaba Mester

See also page 217.

D.L.

How can I say you'll forever be in my thoughts; I hurt to remember. How can I say you'll always be in my heart; I feel heartbroken. How can I say your smile, your faces, your music brings a smile to my face; I feel so sad. How can I say your beautiful soul has now found peace; I want you here with us. How can I think of the dream I had of you a week before you left us knowing you were trying to say something important; I'm sorry I didn't understand.

Chris - I have always felt comforted knowing I could turn to your music, listen to your songs and realize someone else could express in words what I could only feel. You helped me and many others get through this life of uncertainties. You were a constant. Thank you. Now, it's up to me and your fans to return the gift of hope, love and a higher truth to your family, Vicky, Lillian, Toni and Christopher. I promise. Sleep in peace my brother.

DL

Dani V. Brantley

Dearest Chris, I was two years old when "Spoonman" jumped out my television and grabbed me by the ears, forcing me into the *Superunknown*. At that age, I was immediately entangled in Soundgarden's rigorous riffs, liberating licks, and dark yet provocative lyrics. Since that time, I've followed every note, high and low, that you now leave in the airwaves.

When I became old enough to understand what your lyrics meant, it made me go back in time and listen to your previous records. I never knew you, nor did I have the chance to meet you, but somehow with each song, it felt like you knew me. It still feels that way even as I dive into my little box of nostalgia, and listen to the sonic legacy that you, Soundgarden, and Audioslave leave behind. I appreciate your "Loud Love". I cherish you being with me "When I'm Down" and out, in a "Room a Thousand Years Wide". I am in the deepest of gratitude for you telling me to "Be Yourself". You are gone from this plane, but you will forever be my "Last Remaining Light".

To my dearest dark knight, I say thank you.

Signed with loud love, Dani V. Brantley.

Danielle Arthur

It's hard to know where to start. My heart, and spirit, want to thank Chris Cornell. I have always been a huge fan of all of his music. Every band. I loved his solo work so much. As I loved the loud heavy stuff, his solo work spoke to me on such a deep level.

There was always an emotional response. Every range of emotions. Trying to really understand all of his poetic wring has given my heart and mind joy. He truly was an incredible artist on every level.

I will always listen, and hear his beautifully written words forever. His family, friends, and fans have suffered a huge loss. A beautiful genius, who changed so many lives. Eternally grateful.

These words forever.
Danielle.

Darci Mabe

For my 50th birthday I was seeing Soundgarden at the Carolina Rebellion 2013. It got rained out, it was a gusher. Stood out in the rain at the rail for all those bands just hoping that I would see them in my state. Unfortunately the show was cancelled and I was devastated. I spent that whole night upset but I was fortunate enough to get on a flight to Atlanta to see two shows back-to-back the next day.

Lo and behold, as I'm waiting to take my seat, three men walked up and was waiting at the gate. As I looked up, my mind stopped. I knew these faces but I could not utter their names. As I looked at one tall gentleman, I looked over and there was another tall gentleman. I heard in my head *there's Chris Cornell*. No more than five feet from me there's Ben Shepherd. Before I knew it, I was standing in front of them.

Ben said "I like your hat". It was a Seattle hat. I replied "You know it". I then proceeded to ask the guys what happened to them yesterday at the Rebellion, they never showed, kiddingly. Ben says "We bumped that shit, of course, because it was raining so bad". Chris being the media PR man said "No, our plane was delayed. Our plane was delayed," but he stated it very quickly to correct Ben. I said "That's okay, you can redeem yourself. I will see you in Atlanta for the two shows."

I then go back and sit down dazed. I forgot that was the time that Peter, Chris's brother, was in a severe accident so I found myself once again floating over to these people I love so dearly in the rock world, and I said to Chris "My condolences concerning Peters accident". Chris's eyes got really wide like a deer in headlights and he looked at me like *how did you know*? Ben then said "What's happening to Peter?" They started discussing it. Chris said thank you.

We get on the plane and they're sitting in first class, of course, and I walked by them. I could only think of how beautiful these two people were in my life at that time. I went and sat in my seat and all I could do was tell the people around me who was on the plane and some actually knew who they were.

I thought I would not see them anymore until the show. I get off the plane and they are sitting outside waiting on concierge. Ben recognized me with my hat and waved at me and I walked over to them. He was smoking a cigarette while Chris was sitting in the metal chair. Ben was very talkative and very extroverted while Chris kept looking at the ground and really didn't say much. I said to Chris "You are aware that your brother is making a CD called *Champion*?" He said "Yes, I am. Matter of fact we worked on that in my studio at my home."

I was so exhausted from being in 42 degree weather, windy black clouds and raining crocodile tears the previous day. I reached into my folder pulled a flyer out with Peter Cornell's Champion all over it and handed it to Chris. I said "It would be great if you promoted him on your page." I was shaking uncontrollably when I handed it to him. I asked Chris about Toni his mother-in-law and that I miss her on Twitter and she had been sort of silent around that time. He made small talk and said sometimes she just gets tired of being on the internet.

Their concierge finally pulled up. I said "I will see you at the rail. You better recognize I'm a true fan, when I get my pay checks they're written out to Soundgarden instead of me." They sorta laughed and were gone. Sure enough when I was at the concert Ben did his bow and welcomed me, and Chris shook my hand. I was so close to him. I had requested them to play "Mailman". Matt started playing it, pointed his stick at me and he said "That's for you, happy birthday."

Never have I loved or believed in a band as I do Soundgarden and Chris Cornell. This band lead me to so many people from all over the world that shared in a telepathic understanding of the power this man and his music/band held over his fans. Christopher John Cornell. Thank you endlessly.

David E. Dickinson

L.A. Temple Of The Dog - I had a third row right side seat. I talked to a security before the opening act. Told him I had been at the San Francisco concert two nights earlier and he asked if it was good. Partially through the opening act he walked up to me and gestured with his finger to follow him. I said "what's up?" He said "I've been told I can do this and you're first." He took me to center stage on the fence directly in front of Chris' mike. TOTD came out. Chris sang a couple songs and paused. He looked down at me and then scanned the first few rows. "It looks like we have a few friends here tonight".

After it was over, I asked for the setlist from a stagehand. He had McCready's in his hand. He said "no, it's already promised" and gave it to someone. He then walked over to Chris' setlist, picked it up and gave it to me. It is framed on my wall. Yes Chris. You have a few friends here tonight, and they miss you.

Dawn Belotti

It took a while before I was able to go through my endless Soundgarden, Songbook, Higher Truth, Temple Of The Dog albums and choose what could represent my history of photographing Chris Cornell. This is still too painful for me to fully accept but I am starting to heal.

Photo: Dawn Belotti. Carnegie Hall, November 21, 2011.

I first saw Soundgarden, live in 1989, in a tiny NYC club called the Zone DK. This sparked a three-decade love affair with this band. They were the first band I traveled to see. Seattle, Los Angeles, Houston etc. Over the years I had seen the band 56 times. They would swing through a city and play 4-5 shows with a different set list every night. I made friends in many states who I am still close with.

The tattoo was a bad 1990's decision. After having my appendix out and another surgery, the surgeons cut through it. My tattoo artist touched it up and made it bigger. That thing hurt like a bitch.

I first met Cornell in the early 2000's when I was hired by Danny Clinch to produce his John Varvatos shoots. Chris Cornell was a soft-spoken gentleman who passed around photos of his new baby, spoke about how much he missed Seattle and that he was an aspiring chef. I was quite surprised when he ordered chicken fingers for lunch!

I ran into him at an event years later. The man had a memory like an elephant. He liked me, and my company was hired for several projects throughout the years. One time I said I was going to a show in PA. He said to contact an individual and we would be on his list with backstage passes. I was skeptical, but he came through and my friend Bill Burns and I had an amazing time.

When I started writing again, I wanted to write a piece on him for Steel Notes Magazine. A lot of plans fell through and I had to go to Oregon. However when I tweeted the article, I received a heartfelt thank you from the Cornells.

You don't know what someone's life is like unless you live if for yourself. Enjoy every moment of your own.

THANK YOU: A TRIBUTE TO CHRIS CORNELL

BY THE FANS AND FRIENDS OF CHRIS CORNELL

Photo: Dawn Belotti

With Soundgarden, Terminal 5, January 16, 2013.

(For more photos by Dawn Belotti, see front cover and pages 23, 49, 133, 163, 167, 237, 239, 266, 281, 398, 409 and 423.)

Dawn Carroll

You are the shape of the hole in my heart.
  RIP sweet angel.
  Prayers and blessings to your family and loved ones.

de Vie weinstock

Entering the Deathless

He rounds the corner
With his lights on.
In the finale, all he can do is
Embrace the moment.
The light floods in.

The light floods in, and
His love remains, as it has.
The love, that bond he has created in himself,
Is still there, pulsing into the light.
That devotion does not die.

That devotion does not die,
And the devotion will not die.
Because the devotion enters the deathless.

In the shock, there is also the touch of

THANK YOU: A TRIBUTE TO CHRIS CORNELL

The mystery.
All the things we will never know.
We can get a sense of some things:
The war of the world for example:
The war of dark forces against the light,
But nonetheless
Here in the space
There is this potency
Of being with the unknown,
Of the light being with the unknown,
And the movement of it.

Some know who this soul was and others don't.
Some felt moved but didn't know why.
Either way, now
Despite the finality
His spirit has gone into the wind
It circles the earth
Still singing through the vibration of sound
As well as in a fertile fragrant silence
That one can feel
And know as real.

(c) 2017 de Vie weinstock

A Secret Testimony

You take death in your arms like a baby.
That's how loving you are.
You hold it in your arms.
You don't even say no to death.

When the news hits,
The world explodes — or implodes?
The shock and grief are like an explosion though:
A collective "no" —
At least for those of us who
Know you.

Trying to make sense of it
The light still spills all around
Your light even brighter now
Resounding even more
The blazing music surging out even more;

We need to search for the truth.
Even if we never know it completely,
Or if it is impossible to know completely,
We need to search for it.
For the light of truth.

You hold death in your arms like a baby
You don't even say no to it
Despite the reason:
Despite the unnerving trigger point:
Despite the cruel and corrupt instigating factor:
The tyranny of a world gone mad that still kills its prophets,

THANK YOU: A TRIBUTE TO CHRIS CORNELL

You have nonetheless
Married your holy wind of breath even into death
I know this
I know you held that secret testimony
Even in the final moments of body
Until the light
Flooded everywhere
And all you could taste
Was the silent explosion of freedom.

© 2017 de Vie weinstock

Deanna Lynn

Why has this been so painful? Because he was our voice. He sang what we were all feeling, more eloquently than we could speak it. We have not just lost a musician, we have lost a brother. I hope for the best for his family and close friends, as well as his fans. Rest In Peace, brother. May you fly high and watch over us all.

THANK YOU: A TRIBUTE TO CHRIS CORNELL

Photo: Piera Alessio

Debbie Abrams Moore

Came to the earth under the same moon
Never knowing one another
Still you pulled me from despair
Your words struck my heart, a bolt of light
and let it bleed.
Through all of our years you sang for me
Precious moments in my life.
Falling in love, two lovers stargazing in a field
while your words played to us.
It let me dream, it let me scream.
Year after year the voice never failed me
Wisdom with scars for us both came with time
Both fighting for the same cause
To make it to the finish line
A single note transports me back to those days of my youth
Your poetry, your artistry of the heart,
words painted till the end of time
Then suddenly, roaring winds rose from the sea blew out your candle
forced you across your finish line.

THANK YOU: A TRIBUTE TO CHRIS CORNELL

I'll never know where you came from
Had to be another space in time
Where diamonds are created so rare, so fine
never duplicated and just one that came to shine
Gratitude and love in my sadness is what I'm sending to you
Never forgetting all you left for me to use
So be free, travel far and soar high
Imprinted footsteps of your boots across all hearts and minds
Never to be erased, will withstand for all human race
A painter of hearts, only legends are made.

Christopher Cornell, the master, rest in peace.
1964 – 2017.

Sincere love and appreciation,
Debbie Abrams Moore.

Deborah Levesque

When Chris left this earth, there was a silence that took his place. A silence that brought awareness that life is precious and fragile. A sadness for those who are left wondering why.

Desda Sayer

Such a tragic loss! Thankful for his beautiful, musical contributions to the world. It brought back feelings of when we lost Kurt. I still remember that day and how empty/sad that I felt. The same feelings arose with the news of Chris. A good portion of us grew up during the "grunge" era and Chris was a part of our history our story. I had to go and listen to Audioslave today... "I Am the Highway" and I broke into tears. So fucking sad!

From Seattle... I'm sending all my love, light and positivity to his family and to all of the fans! Music will never be the same without you! Rest easy Chris! Much love to you all.

Desiree Jo Ruiz

This seriously sucks! Now what? He is the greatest vocalist/musician of all time, at least in all MY time. His voice was the sound of an angel... There really is no one to compare?

23 years I followed up on him. Every new person I met, someway, somehow, I brought him into the conversation! I could do the same but this time... I dunno? It'll be different? It won't be with that excitement and eagerness to see him at his next show, or running to the television to record the next talk show he is going to make an appearance on, or that complete excitement to buy the next new album, or watch a movie ONLY because he is on the soundtrack! Or to look for tickets on 1iota anticipating his next appearance (you guys know what I'm talking about?) NOW WHAT!!!???

Many have said this "His music has been the soundtrack of my life!" This holds true in regards to my life as well! I discovered him the summer before I started high school. I'll never ever forget that day! I was watching MTV, in Arkansas (my first trip away from home) in my teens, discovering my independence. That morning, the instant I heard his voice I knew he was going to be a part of my everyday life! That's exactly where he's been from that day forward! Every big moment, every broken moment and all those in between! (without his knowledge of it!) lol he was there! If and when I ever get married this song [Finally Forever] I hoped to play... Hmmm, I guess that's what I could look forward to? Right?? Who am I kidding? I could have never have pulled it off somehow, actually having him sing this song at my wedding!!? LOL Although, that was my BIG DREAM! Don't laugh ! This is serious! But ya know? You guys get it? Right?? I have this spot etched in my soul reserved only for his music.

"Music is that ray of light in every dark moment " Chris Cornell's music has been and will forever be that ray of light... if only I could have conveyed this to him? If only he could have really seen and understood the impact he's made in our lives. Like him, I suffered the same. Depression/addiction are two of the biggest mountains to climb! As a human from one to another... if I only I could have discussed this with him? Would it have changed the outcome? Just a little? I'm only one little person in this big world... who knows? This big world is full of possibilities and with my higher power who I call "God", all things are possible?

What I'm trying to say is that I'm extremely sad about this. He will be forever in my soul, forever missed forever adored, by little ole me.

Diane McDonald-Topping

There is a hole in my soul that will never be filled; such emptiness left by his passing. My heart is shattered into a million little pieces.

Chris Cornell was a blindingly brilliant talent whose lifelight was extinguished far too soon; a humble and gentle man, beautiful inside and out, leaving a legacy that will live forever in our minds and in our hearts.

That one brief moment of walking on air because we got talking on Twitter; me, a nobody from Melbourne, Australia, alone in the office in the early hours of the morning; him suffering from insomnia, about how we both loved to smoke but had given it up but some days still craved that deep inhalation and the rush it brought and how he'd taken up guitar playing to keep his fingers busy; about the lyrics to Men At Work's "Downunder" and the meaning of the word 'chunder'; of the 13 year drought we were suffering from at the time; how if it wasn't for the fans he would still be cleaning fish in restaurants; of not recognising me because I'd changed my avatar so I changed it back; of offering free VIP passes to any of his shows if we came over; of going to the show at the Wiltern on 3 May 2009, going backstage and Pete Thorn saying 'Oh, you're the ones! He's been talking about you guys' because we'd flown from Melbourne to see him and the band perform and standing three feet away from Brad Pit, BRAD PITT, and not saying anything because I was too shy and didn't want to intrude.

How lucky was I to see him perform in all his different guises; from Audioslave on 26th April 2003; to Soundgarden at the Gorge 30th July 2011; to his Songbook tours; to Temple of the Dog twice in San Francisco on 10th and 11th November 2016; and finally meeting him in Melbourne on 3rd December 2015, and him saying that I looked familiar and that he remembered the Wiltern gig from 2009; the slight tinge of regret in his voice because he'd given his Triumph to Peter, not for the gift but for the 'what ifs', and the hug, a real tight hug and saying 'Thank you' and me saying 'No, thank you'. He re-awaken my love of music all on his own because of who he was; to the people I've met and the things that I've done if it wasn't for him. Thank you is not enough.

That one brief moment of walking on air; there is a hole in my soul that will never be filled; such is the emptiness left by his passing.

I hope he is at peace now and forever.

Doc Thomas

Brother, Father, Husband, Bandmate, Friend, Smart Ass, Mentor, Inspiration, Muse, Composer, Gifted, Rock God, Genre Architect, Philanthropist, Beacon of hope, and a million other things to a million other people.

But right now, by crooked steps, he is the hole inside my heart.

A little background about me: I was born into Soul, Funk, and early Hip-Hop; raised by Blues, Jazz, Metal, and 'Grunge'; and currently live by whatever song oozes from my fingers or drips from my lips. In an existence where the only constant is change, music remains the ubiquitous entity able to skate around the variable constant as a helix, shifting sounds with time yet always unapologetically present.

Somewhere along the way, I gravitated toward the vibes emanating from Alice In Chains and Soundgarden. Their music contained elements of my upbringing infused with crashing guitars, thunderous rhythms, off-kilter time signatures, introspective brooding, and preternatural voices that will haunt me for the rest of my life. Little did I know their respective lyrics and writing styles would become some of the most crucial navigational charts I would ever use to weather future storms. Or to what extent their influence would indelibly affect my creative calibre.

Jerry Cantrell and Chris Cornell, The Bear and The Snake as I like to call them, are two ever-present slices of the eight-part collective. As a songwriting guitarist, it's only natural I would grow fondly attached to them both. Jerry's approach to writing, with his esoteric metaphors and wordplay, has a brutally honest way of telling it like it is. His vocal harmonies with Layne Staley reverberated into my bones, forcing me to own up and face whatever particular truth I was fighting so hard to deny at the time. Chris's approach, also equally clever, would confirm said ugly truth. His voice, however; be it banshee wail or velvet croon, was the poignant reminder that everything would eventually be okay. A simple reminder that I already had the strength to overcome anything. Be it rough seas or smooth sailing, band efforts or solo projects, neither one has ever let me down.

A fracture happened. After the release of *Down On The Upside*, Soundgarden broke up. Like a kid in the middle of a proverbial divorce, my attentions went primarily toward AIC and Jerry's first solo record, *Boggy Depot*. I visited Chris with his *Euphoria Mourning* record (and later Audioslave) on weekends. Jerry got me through the end of high school; the devastating loss of Layne Staley (the then conclusion of Alice In Chains); the first couple of college years; mortuary school; and the shit show that was my life between 2005 and the beginning of 2009.

Fast forward to 2013. Out of the blue, I had an unyielding desire to hear Chris's voice. I took my mp3 player and set everything I had of his on it to a playlist. I'd fallen in love all over again. To my disappointment, the digital collection only contained *Superunknown*, *King Animal*, one single from *Euphoria Mourning* and two singles from Audioslave's first record. I dug up old tapes and CDs, even ordering a few replacements to refill the discography tank. From the radio, other cars at stoplights, at the pub, over store PAs, to movie soundtracks, that distinctive siren call began to follow me everywhere. "Okay Chris, you've got me. I'm listening. What are you trying to say?"

In April 2014, there was a karaoke party at a local recording studio. I sang "Fell On Black Days", the sobering anthem that often comforted me during beatdowns of unexplainable sadness. From there, I was invited back a few more times and recorded a few extra covers before being encouraged to start bringing in original material. Somehow spending time in the studio opened the floodgates wide enough to decimate a decade long writer's block. Chris's *Scream* and *Songbook* records suddenly became the soundtrack of an endless summer that me lead on an unprecedented whirlwind road trip to NYC where I found Bleecker Street Zeke (the infamous 6-stringed love of my life); to NJ where I finally wrote a second verse to a song I'd started in 2005; to VA Beach for a continued celebration of Soundgarden's reunion and 20th anniversary of *Superunknown*, and back home to numerous local shows in between everything else. Working up the gumption to try out my new material for the inaugural attempt at open mic should have been a fitting conclusion to an exciting year. Yet a dark cloud of unfulfilled longing lingered.

While sitting in the kitchen one evening, knee deep in a research paper and mindless listening to *Scream*, I heard somebody say "Get up!" Frustrated at the audacity of interruption, I unburied my head from my work and loudly retorted "What!?" It took a moment to realise I'd just yelled at the stereo. Unphased by the outburst, Chris went on to sing [about getting up off the floor and doing something]. That was it. I replayed track four. Every word eerily paralleled my life at present. Who would've guessed the record many wagered would be the musical undoing of the great Cornell would turn out to be the conduit of my reawakening.

In January 2015, my long time friend and vocal coach, Kriston, suggested I enter NPR's Tiny Desk Contest. I, along with a few thousand others, lost to Fantastic Negrito (and rightfully so). His dirty grit sound reminded me of my own and his story inspired me to keep pushing forward; to, as he would later pen, "Hump Through the Winter". So I did. No fucks

THANK YOU: A TRIBUTE TO CHRIS CORNELL

Photo: Doc Thomas

(For more photos, see pages 43, 129 and 193.)

given. We became friends on Twitter and I've been following his work ever since.

By May, I had gone into the studio to record my debut solo effort with no label support, no budget for session musicians, and no time to wait on anyone. The dog days of August brought the first official Dirty Metal Lefty gig; however, the crisp airs of autumn would be the moment of truth. "Nevá On Sunday" dropped on October 16. Two days prior to release, I drove to Rockville, MD to see Chris during the first run of the *Higher Truth* tour. I left an advanced copy of my CD on stage before the show started, not so much for him but more so for me. As a matter of fact, he almost stepped on it during a Bob Dylan cover. That didn't matter because the gesture was meant to signify finality, a turning point if you will. I had crossed the rubicon heading toward how I'd plan to occupy the rest of my days.

2016 brought more gigs around town and shot Fantastic Negrito's career into the stratosphere. To my pleasant surprise, Chris tapped him to open on the European leg of Higher Truth's second run. I'd never been more proud, truly a win for every indie artist working to crawl out of the underground. Not long after, local punk band, The Weak Days, picked me up to hit the road with them too. Dirty Metal Lefty jumped out of the fish bowl. The highway offered new fans, new friends, and long hours of reflective contemplations. Negrito told me he didn't know for certain if he would continue his residence as opener for the North American dates so, I got to thinking. . . No fucks given. . . and placed a one-time bid for the slot when the tour stopped in Richmond, VA. The tour folks actually followed up expeditiously. Turns out Negrito would in fact stay on to finish out the rest of his tenure.

If you've never had an opportunity see Chris Cornell live in any capacity, then you have my genuine sympathies. YouTube videos and concert footage don't quite do the experience justice. The rock shows will keep you out of your seat, leaving you elevated with ringing ears and a hoarse voice. The acoustic gigs are a completely different monster entirely. I felt more in tune with those since I could relate to the unnerving quiet of being on stage armed with only a guitar and the timbre of your own voice. Exposed and raw. All of your vulnerabilities lay bare to the mercy of an unforgiving (and at times, intoxicated) audience. But he did it. He gave us his all seemingly with little to no effort, room by room, night after night. I swear, that man could sing the dictionary or the federal tax code and I would buy it no questions asked.

The aura of his presence is physically palpable. I guess that sort of thing happens from candidly sharing your soul with the world for over three decades. Before he utters a word, you feel as if you already know him. In a way, everybody knows him — especially when Chris the Human would slip out in between vocal melodies with his uncanny penchant for the lost art of storytelling. He'd regale us with the origins of our favourite songs, tales from the road, hilarious audience banter, ancedotes of fatherhood and how his wife is smarter than he is, or even occasional commentary on the news of the day. Some days I'd wish he would sit down to write a book of his musings.

Then it happened. One more item marked off the grocery list dreams and personal goals. I met him in Albany, NY (shout out to Linda for helping to make that happen). Maybe he remembered me from the show two nights before or maybe not. Who cares? Nevertheless, it was like catching up with an old friend. I mentioned how "The sun never sets on a badass." and his face lit up. What I remember most is his hug. My head rested briefly in the crux of a branch-like limb affixed to the trunk on a redwood of a man. (Due to our height difference, I only came up to his armpit.) The single embrace drained from me every morsel of negative energy, every bit of stress, every residual scrap of unrelated malcontent; allowing room for a fleeting moment of total zen. That shit was magical!

Celebrity aside, I am inclined to believe the prodigious occurrence is a testament of his ever evolving empathetic character. Here was someone who'd braved the trenches, buried friends before their time, fought numerous battles against personal demons and WON; someone who made a point to use his position of influence to act on his own sense of personal responsibility through philanthropy and other altruistic undertakings.

Here was a man who had found his peace. Fates rest the souls of Andy, Layne, Shannon, Kurt, Jeff, Michael, Whitney, Prince, the others who have fallen on the journey. Through every stumble, he always lived to sing and play another day. That's what makes Chris's passing so difficult to fathom. We grew up with him. He was supposed to make it. He was supposed to die a gregarious old man still on top of his game, surrounded by loved ones and respected by all as the best to ever do it.

The trouble with finding peace is realising how much harder we have to work to hold on to it; perhaps even harder than the initial efforts to find it. Peace is elusive. It is the rain that slips between our fingers on a hot day. Even if we cup our hands to catch it, it can still spill over our palms out of our grasp when we're not careful. Thus peace is also precious. As I sit here, hours before his burial, weeping over the night he flew away, weeping for the song we'll never write together, the stage we'll never share, the bands he'll never play with again, the light of a candle extinguished too soon, the unforgettable hug that could easily eradicate cancer or at least my need for morning caffeine; my grief is deeply humbled by the fact that those hugs were probably a duty free routine for Chris's wife Vicky and his three beautiful children. I can't begin to comprehend the volatile tempest surrounding his family and close friends. I weep for them. I weep for Peter. I weep Ben, Kim, and Matt. For Eddie. For Tom, Tim, and Brad. I weep for the bonds of their brotherhood forged by blood and cemented in the music that keeps them together. I weep for the prospect of being forced to carry on with questions no one may ever have an answer to.

I refuse to offer any farewells or goodbyes because through us, the great Cornell is immortal. Instead, I am thankful. I raise my glass to the memories, to the friendships born from shared appreciation and admiration, to the Black Hole Sons conceived during "Black Hole Sun", for getting us into trouble while keeping us out of it, for giving us the patience to keep calm and keep on rowing, to the Drop Ds, to the 6/8s and the 3/4s, to the laughs, the humility, the humanity, the middle fingers, to Chris spending the better half of 32 years without a shirt, to tears shed, to autographs, to searching all over town for a desired bootleg import, to standing in rain after a long drive to see the band, to the perfect combination of pizza and music videos, to a smile that continues to melt the shattered fragments of a broken heart, to charitable deeds, to social awareness, to understanding the world extends further than yourself, to the legacy left behind.

But still I weep. And I pray. May the weight we schlep on our hearts grow lighter with each passing step. As we commit his body to the earth today, let us not forget each other in the violet hours of the coming months for grief knows nothing of linear timelines. Listen closely in your moments of despair. Listen for that distinctive siren call. Chris has never let us down before and I don't see any reason he would do so now.

Peace & Blessings, Loud Love, Cheers
-"Dirty" Doc Thomas
(Dirty Metal Lefty)

Donna Barton

Three and a half years ago I started a page called Chris Cornell A Legend in His Own Time and it has been growing and I have gotten to know some of the people who run other Chris pages and they are the best.

    A couple of years ago, I told my hubby that my last dying wish was to see Chris, and this was right after Soundgarden had just reunited, so to my surprise when they were scheduled to be here in Dallas, my husband handed my a ticket to see him, and the venue was general admission, standing room only, so I realised that I would have to find a wheelchair, because I would never be able to stand that long. I was able to get three rows of people in front of the stage. I was so close, but was heartbroken because I could not see him with people standing in front of me. I might have been heartbroken but was still grateful for getting to go. And have decided that "Say Hello to Heaven" will be played at my funeral. The best part of this is I know I will see him again someday, one on one. Till then, Chris.

Dora Guadalupe Zalazar

Who would tell me in August of 1992 that I would love that guy so much... that I'd be feeling this pain so deep...

Doug Daigle

On a recent road trip, my nine year old daughter, Elizabeth, sings word for word "I Am The Highway", and "Can't Change Me", as beautiful as I've ever heard and immediately follows with a stern request for "Black Hole Sun"... brought tears of joy down my face. My memories with Chris and SG are long and deep but passing his music on to the next generation may be the sweetest. Heart heavy missing him.

Emilio Di Tullio

First family trip of the summer and my wife says, "can you play something else, I don't thing I can handle Chris Cornell right now." I turned off the music and took a moment...

Then I said, "I don't think you understand, I don't have anything else."

Emily Wagner

The Day I Met Chris Cornell

Regina, SK 7/26/16

This day did not come easy let me say that! First of all, it's 25 years in the making.

    I can't remember the exact moment I first saw and heard Chris Cornell, but I know it was early high school, circa 1990. Ever since then I've been listening, and watching. I remember playing the Soundgarden *Flower* EP in my cassette player during downtime in class. I remember watching (and recording) Headbangers Ball. I remember that concert a long time ago at the Unicorn (which used to be an old grocery store), Chris Cornell stage diving RIGHT over me and nearly falling on me! I remember his scenes in *Singles*, which remains my favorite movie to this day, and not just because of Chris. It's a timeless movie with great music and plot! A chick flick with kickass music. What more could you want? I remember Lollapolooza at the Fort Bend Fairgrounds... the mud, sweat and tears!

    Then Soundgarden broke up. Now what?

    It was a bad dream, but I still had the music to listen to,

Soundgarden, Temple of the Dog and a little solo stuff ("Sunshower"). Then Chris came out with his first solo album, releasing *Euphoria Morning* and I fell in love all over again… and again and again with *Carry On*, *Songbook*, *Scream* and later with Audioslave. He cut his hair, and I still loved him, realizing it wasn't about the looks, it was the SOUND. The voice, the lyrics, the music. All about the music (ok, and a little looks). I saw him solo for the Euphoria Morning and Scream tour. I barely remember the Euphoria Morning tour, but I DO remember that someone I knew was gonna get me a backstage pass, and I missed the call. That was the closest I'd ever come to meeting him. Life goes on…

Soundgarden re-united and I saw them twice, both times from far away in large arenas, nothing like the intimate setting where I saw the Scream tour… standing just feet from the stage. I missed his Songbook stop in Houston, because tickets sold out in seconds and I was unaware of sites like Stubhub back then. I also never saw Audioslave because they always played at festivals I never wanted to attend.

September 2015, *Higher Truth* release… I'll be honest, I didn't really know Chris was even working on this album until shortly before its release. I heard an NPR piece about it, including an interview and some snippets of the songs. Wow. At that moment, I wanted it badly. After it came in the mail, I put it in the car, iPod and iTunes and it's been on repeat ever since! No joke. I have to listen EVERY DAY, or the world is not right. I knew Chris would tour. Got tickets to Dallas on my birthday, then Houston (where I waited outside in the cold rain for over an hour after the show in hopes of running into him), St. Louis, then Charlotte. Something told me it wasn't over. And it wasn't.

I knew Chris offered meet and greets (including two tickets) through IfOnly.com. I had checked there periodically, and he didn't offer any the first leg of the tour, but then he offered them up for the second leg. I thought about it briefly for Charlotte, but before I could take a bite, they were gone. Then in July I checked again. To torture myself. And lo and behold... I scroll down reading "sold out" again and again and again, then wait a minute! One available for Regina, Canada. WTF!!! Could it be? Where the fuck is Regina (pronounced RE-gyna BTW)? (head over to Google Maps). I clicked "purchase" and put it in the cart, then left the computer, thinking what if? But it'll be gone soon anyway, so why think about it.

The next morning I woke up with a reminder email about the purchase in my cart. It's still there! No way! Almost instinctively, and impulsively, I continued the transaction. I had seen Chris perform four separate times this tour... And now was the time to finally meet him. I was in the mountains with VERY spotty internet connection, so it took awhile... a couple of attempts. Then BAM. Purchased. Holy shit! Now what!? I got very excited, then thought, who is gonna come with me to this? I hurried to FB where I frantically put out the feelers. Not one bite! Everyone who wanted to had already met him and was out of money – due to traveling to see him like me, etc. No matter. I pushed on, my mind literally SPINNING with the idea that I would meet Chris. I refused to believe it, though, until all the logistics were worked out, and even until the second before he walked into the room, but I will get to that later.

I scrambled to try to book a flight to Regina fucking Canada. Found one. Booked. The next day, or after, I can't remember, I realized I booked the trip for the WRONG DAY!!! OMG!!!! It must have been due to contracting the very rare disease called "Going to meet my favorite rock star amnesia." So I had to call and cancel and re-book. I spent like two hours on my dearly "dead" phone, in a van traveling across country. I was in the backseat and had to scramble to plug my phone up front so it wouldn't lose the charge during the phone call (while my step dad drove!). Unbelievable, but got it straightened out.

Then, the more I thought about it I realized the trip is in CANADA! I had no idea where my passport was. I was out of state and couldn't search. Plus, I remember the last time I saw it (God knows when) it was expired! AHHH! Frantically started searching for how to expedite. When I got home I tore the whole place up looking for it, and finally found it, after several rounds with the passport expediting company. I had to gather SEVERAL documents, including a newly ordered birth certificate, and mail them off. It took like two days and several hundred dollars (more). SHIT! Oh, and I failed to mention that the weekend BEFORE the Canada trip, I had already booked ANOTHER trip to see another concert with a friend out of state!!! So... I had to cancel that and... even worse had to call her to tell her I wasn't coming, because, well, I was going to MEET Chris Cornell. FUCK!

After all the travel was booked, background check completed from ifonly.com, and hotel.... I sat back and waited. The passport arrived and it really started feeling real. Thinking of the moment made my heart race.... Literally. What would I say/do when I saw him? I only had five minutes! Would I remember everything? What would he say? What would I get him to sign/give him! OMG the thoughts were endless...

Fast forward to July 25, 2016... Day of departure. Bags packed, leaving behind a condo in utter disarray from painting and renovating, I headed to Bush Intercontinental. Remember all my previous travel headaches? Well, more were coming. The parking lot machine ate my credit card. There were storms in the surrounding area and my plane BARELY took off... We sat there for over an hour... praying the storms wouldn't move in closer! Finally, we're in the air! Once in Canada, I literally RAN to customs, waddled through security and RAN to my gate, where they were announcing final boarding call. What was initially supposed to be a two HOUR layover turned out to be two seconds! I arrived at my hotel at like 1 a.m. and barely slept.

The next afternoon I got a text: "Hi Emily, Martin here. Chris C's security. Please meet me at the merchandise table at 7:30 pm with your guest. Thanks." Shit just got real. And, uh... I don't have a guest. Then I get another text: "Our flight is delayed. Let's meet at 7:45 instead. Don't worry you will definitely meet him before he goes on." Breathe. It's ok...

I gathered my items to bring and walked to the bus stop. I get there no problem... it was a short walk to the Conexus Art Center... however there was NO sidewalk leading directly to it, so I had to poke holes in the grass to get there with my heels! Oh well! I got there just after 6:30 when doors opened. People are starting to trickle in. The front doors are VERY close to the admission area and very small merchandise booth. I give the nice older lady at will-call my last name and she can't find it. I tell her I'm on the band's guest list. God, I felt SO special. This was it! Finally, I get the real fan treatment! I wait for a while and another lady comes out and says they're retrieving my ticket. A short while later she brings it back... It is orchestra row G (13th row) – well I had 4th for Charlotte, so I was a little disappointed, but immensely grateful I wasn't BALCONY!

Then at 7:45: "Just left the airport. Be there soon." Holy shit again. He'll be here soon. I'd been waiting for over an hour, so soon felt so - soon.

Then Martin appeared, who said "There you are. Let's go... follow me," and so it began. I looked at Martin, grasped the items I brought for Chris and walked, one foot in front of the other, up some stairs, weaving through the crowds, dodging dudes juggling beers. Taking deep breaths. Heading through the black doors that lead to the other side where Chris is. Inside it's pitch black and Martin has to shine a light and say watch your step. I mention how nervous I am, and Martin tells me something like – "Don't worry, Chris is really cool." He says we'll find a dressing room and set up. We go to the first one on the left through a narrow hallway. It's small, carpeted and lit with dim florescent. There is a mirrored wall to the left with a long, brown table beside a small, dingy white-tiled shower with a curtain. There's also a toilet straight ahead, with an old-timey white sink in the middle. There are angled mirrors to the right, fashioned in dressing room style, and a small black, mini fridge alongside. Martin grabs two plain, brown cushioned chairs and puts them right in front of each other. The room and space are so small, the chairs so close together.

Then he says he's gonna get Chris. I have to actually remember to breathe. I have to remember to breathe as I write this, 33 hours later. While Martin's away I realize my mouth is so parched. I spy a nearly-empty abandoned water bottle on top of the mini-fridge and desperately debate swigging it, but instead take a quick a drink from the faucet. It's so nasty, but I don't care. I wipe my mouth and look in the mirror. This is it. No time for primping. I turn and moments later, Chris rounds the corner and almost glides into the room, like a Rock God apparition. There he is, standing RIGHT in front of me, hand outstretched. We shake hands and I place my other hand on his and smile. He hugs me. Wow. We sit. The items I brought for autographs are next to us on the table. And before I know it, I look over the door is mostly CLOSED and we're sitting, directly in front of each other in this tiny space, just the TWO of us! Chris Cornell and I are alone, although very briefly. I had him ALL to myself, contained, no one else around! How cool is that! What did we talk about? It's kind of a blur, but here's the gist.

I told him I'm from Texas, and explained that this is my fifth concert this tour and that I came to Regina because it was the only meet and greet left. We talked about Canada and he told me that growing up in Seattle, he came to go fishing a lot when he was younger with his dad. I (think) I told him I went to Banff for my honeymoon and mentioned seeing the Canadian Rockies from the plane this trip. During what seemed like a lull in conversation, I told him *Higher Truth* truly touched my soul and I just had to meet him to tell him that IN PERSON. It was the real reason I was there. I wished him a happy, belated birthday and congratulations on the wonderful tour. He smiled and said thanks, his eyes twinkling behind his glasses. I told him my son loves to sing his stuff and showed him a video of Rowan singing "Nearly Forgot My Broken Heart". I know my son sings at least three songs – NFMBH, "Josephine" and "Higher Truth", but I could not for the life of me at that moment think of all three! I stumbled and jumbled telling Chris the track names, while trying to find the video. He held my phone and smiled and chuckled softly.

As we're sitting I am just trying to take it ALL in, looking at him without trying to stare, but trying to remember EVERY detail. He had a reddish shirt with little holes scattered all over it, with a shirt underneath. His glasses were dark, with a beautiful greenish tint around the edges. At one point I wanted to compliment him on them, but the moment passed, like several others before and after that. I noticed lots of gray hair in his roots. I noticed a pronounced muscle on his playing arm. His skin was glowing, so smooth. I thought he seemed small, not short (obviously) but small framed, barely any width to him, like I could wrap both arms around him twice! He had greenish pants and big boots on. I noticed his long fingernails (for guitar plucking). He has aged well. Very well. He is truly beautiful. There is just no other way to put it.

So the conversation went on. I asked if he missed his really long hair, and flipping it around. He smiled and said something I can't even remember. I mentioned the Temple of the Dog reunion and that I missed the presale and he said tickets go on sale soon. I gave him his gift, explaining the quote inside the frame. I said I read somewhere that he loves to read and that I picked the quote by Sylvia Plath (his favorite author) because it reminds me to stay in the moment, which I was trying to do JUST then. *"Remember, remember, this is now, and now and now. Live it, feel it, cling to it. I want to become acutely aware of all that I've taken for granted,"* it read. I told him about the letter I wrote to him that's inside the frame, and he turned it over and looked for it. I laughed and said it's inside the frame and he can open it later. Now I wish I would have taken it out. I think he thought it was taped to the back.... He seemed like he wanted to read it right then.

At some point Martin came back in with a gold Sharpie and disappeared... Shortly after Chris picked up my ragged *Higher Truth* CD cover. I remember watching him turning it over in his hands and thinking WOW, he's holding the masterpiece HE created... I think I mentioned to him that I missed the Songbook tour, but so glad I've been able to see Higher Truth. He then said something like he was glad he was able to put out a CD with new songs, because SB was mostly previously released material. He muttered something about Soundgarden re-uniting. I remember him saying that it's impossible to play under two hours because he just has so many songs. All the while, he's talking AND signing his trademark signature, carefully placing the words on the front cover. I can't even remember if I told him my name, and here is signing it, correct spelling and everything! He put the cover down and Martin came back in, then as we're standing up Chris offered to sign my *Singles* DVD cover. I told him it's my favorite movie and he should have won an Oscar for his "brief" role. Both he and Martin grinned.

Martin suggested where to stand for the picture – by the door. We stood so close, he put his arm around my right shoulder and I put mine on his left hip. It all seemed so natural, like we'd met before. I wasn't nervous touching him, but I definitely noticed the feel of him! As I turned to gather my stuff, he bent to hug me very close. His hair was right next to my face and I clung to him gently and breathed his sweet smell in DEEPLY. I told him "thank you. From the bottom of my heart, your music means the world to me. I am a loyal fan forever, thank you so much." He looked at me after that and said "thank you" with such simple sincerity and grace. And then it was over. As I'm being whisked away back to reality, through the darkness and into the light of the theater, I hear Martin call to me, WAIT – here's a guitar pick and he gives it to me. As I exit I see the stage to the left through some curtains and realize I'm "BACKSTAGE"... and I want to stay there. Exiting, I passed by opening act Fantastic Negrito, who I had also just met (along with several other fans) at the merchandise booth. He said "Hey, I know you!" And I giggled like a schoolgirl "I just met Chris!"

I don't want to write about any regrets, because I have none. Sure, I wish I'd talked more about one thing or another. I wish I would have requested a specific song. But none of that matters. I told him what really matters, how much his music and voice mean to me. It all adds up to one of the best, most surreal nights of my life. I kept thinking about it all concert long and crying... tears literally streaming as I thought about that moment (the concert was amazing and is a WHOLE different essay altogether). Tears streaming as I thought to myself, this is the LAST Higher Truth concert I'll see. For real, this time. As I listened to his charming, curse word filled rants, funny stories – stuff like calling Bryan a "gangsta," and hearing his high-pitched wails, I laugh to myself thinking – is this the same calm, collected soft spoken man I JUST met backstage!? And now there's no going back, for I've lived out one of my most amazing dreams and met the most amazing artist, Chris Cornell. Thank you for your grace, and sweet, humble nature. Thanks for the hugs and talk and autographs. It was so worth it.

Thank you, Chris. I will never take this day for granted… I am grateful that it is indeed "our time in the universe." All my (loud) love, Emily

November 7, 2016 Madison Square Garden – Temple of the Dog reunion
(*please note this is NOT edited for factual details. I only used my own poor memory… so if dates are wrong, etc… forgive me!)

25 years ago, I discovered Temple of the Dog. I was a huge fan of Soundgarden… as huge as I could be at 15 years old. I had recently discovered them, but loved them.

1991… a year after lead singer of Mother Love Bone, Andy Wood, died… Temple of the Dog released their one and only self titled 10 track album. I listened. I loved… then I put away. I dusted it off recently, before the announced reunion tour and played it, skipping over several tracks to listen to my perpetual faves – "All Night Thing", "Reach Down", "Call me a Dog" and "Four Walled World". Never in a million years did I expect a reunion tour, but then TOTD re-acquired their demo tapes that had been in litigation for so long… then they did announce a small tour. WOW! I have to go… so I quickly signed up for the fan club presale and got tickets – first to New York City and then Philadelphia (on a whim). I then realized that Philly was a much better (i.e. smaller) venue so begrudgingly decided to sell my NYC tickets. I resigned myself to have the best time possible, coordinating meet-ups with my fellow Chris Cornell fans!

I purchased my tickets months in advance. Work provided

a steady relief of distraction. I almost didn't have TIME to think about this epic event! Then, just a few days before the monumental event (Philly show 2) I started listening to the 25-year anniversary Temple release... NON-STOP... and boy, was I excited!

November 4... I landed in Philly very late at night (ALONE), my 40th birthday just three days before, I arrived glowing with the knowledge that I would soon see and hear Chris again in a matter of hours. Anyone who's known me for two minutes knows my devotion to this man... his talent and poetry.

Temple of the Dog were set to play at the Tower Theater in Upper Darby, a suburb of Philadelphia. They had already played their premier show just the night before... I arrived with a couple of friends (already bonded with them over my mutual love of Chris). We parked... my heart beating quickly, but my mind STILL not quite believing what was to come!

I went to what I thought was my assigned seat to watch opening act, Fantastic Negrito and if you haven't checked this talented dude out yet, hurry up! After a few songs, I decided to move closer to the stage, ending up behind some raucous young men in plaid (not flannel) shirts. I decided to move closer yet again, ultimately ending up on row EE – fitting because my first name is EMILY... and I thought deservingly so due to my recent 40th birthday. Technically this was 5th row... 15 rows ahead of what I had purchased, but I figured what the heck. I would at least try to stick it out whole show! I called my traveling buddy, who quickly agreed to sneak down to sit next to me from her balcony seats. It worked! No one ever came to claim these high quality floor seats!

I rocked on the whole night through... 25 songs. Amazing. It was the perfect mix of Temple of the Dog, Mother Love Bone and appropriate (fun) covers. Wow! The younger girl standing next to me, and rocking out, didn't know some songs, so I filled her in with a full heart! She was so excited!

I sung so hard and loud that night, I thought my voice would never recover... and it still quite hasn't. HA! "Pushing

Forward Back" provided me with much more energy than anticipated. I always liked that song, but sometimes skipped over it in CD-land. But it provided surprising energy live. I screamed along. The Tower provided me, and most others, with a raw energy... such a small place... like a dive bar. It was perfect for a Temple of the Dog reunion 25 years later. Black folding chairs linked together lined the floor. Narrow rows with sticky floors greeted guests as if saying "Hello. This is what is WAS like more than two decades ago, or what would have been."

Chris and company played for well over two hours, making me wish I really HAD worn a Depends undergarment for the show! However, I did make it out to the bathroom during one unknown song. I made sure I ran back as to not miss any pivotal moment!

After two encores including "Man of Golden Words"... a cover that makes me think of both Chris AND Andy's lyrical abilities... and some surprising covers including "Fascination Street" by The Cure, the show ended as quickly as it had begun... but not before the five members gathered arm in arm on stage in unison. Wow. I clapped, cheered, yelled for dead life along with other fans. What a stunning reunion. I would have cried had I not known I would see them again just days later!

After a brief, exhausted tour of Philly, my co-fans and me packed it up to head to the Big Apple where Temple would be playing no else than Madison Square Garden. My online friend had generously gifted me a ticket. Where were my seats? I didn't know and it really didn't matter! My crew got there mid afternoon and settled in to meet some other fans, which we did eventually. It was great camaraderie! A chance to meet other hard-core fans! What seemed like minutes later it was time to head down to MSG... walking in the brisk New York air, my excitement grew, but I didn't expect it to be as great as Philly – fifth row!

They started, as they had on other nights, with an instrumental of "Man of Golden Words". A song I CANNOT get out of my head since then. Then they blasted into "Say Hello to Heaven", a direct tribute to the late Andy Wood. I'm writing this not as a review really. I don't need to analyze every song, whether or not Chris hit the high notes. What I do remember is the energy. I sang to every song loudly (as I always do). I stood the whole time. No one told me to be quiet (as they have done at solo Chris shows) and no one told me to sit down. In fact, the dude in front of me kept singing with me and high-fiving me throughout the show. At one point I remember apologizing and he praised me for my enthusiasm! Wow! What a concept ;)

Just before the show started my brother, who lives in New York, told me he'd be attending the show with a friend. Now, my brother isn't really a fan, but he always has connections. I told him we should meet up. At one point I texted him and told him I'm coming down to his seats. At that point I headed down to the section just below. When I arrived at the door there stood a fragile-looking old man who asked for my tickets. I quietly told him I didn't have seats for this section, but I REALLY wanted to meet up with my brother. I even said please. The old guy looked at me so sweetly. He didn't say no, but I knew what he meant. I kept saying please and then he whispered that his boss was right there. I saw her walk by and I just said out loud – well I'm gonna go on down and walked right in. Hopefully, I didn't get him in trouble.

Once inside I stood on an aisle seat... just one section down was amazing. I could see so much better! I sang along, then shortly after that my brother met up with me. Just before he'd texted about his amazement of Chris's voice. Was there any doubt? We walked down the aisle to where his friend sat. The show ended shortly after that. It was then his friend said "let's head down". "Down where?" I thought to myself. Come to find out it's BACKSTAGE.

My brother, without thinking, takes off HIS VIP sticker and gives it to me. I, without thinking, start to head down and realize he can't come and the guilt overpowers me. But the idea of going backstage overpowered that feeling instantaneously.

My brother stood in the stands as I turned my back and headed down. What a selfless act!

Going down his friend told me the rules: Don't act like a fan. Keep it cool. Follow my lead. Uh... of course! As I'm following the crowd through a narrow tunnel leading to several different rooms backstage I barely have time to think about what's happening. It's late. I'm exhausted, my head spinning from the amazing musical journey I've been on. As I round a corner I spot Vicky Cornell in the corner of my eye, laughing in a doorway. I keep walking, trying to contain myself. Keep it cool.

We end up in a small room with a few standing room tables and benches. We get a drink and sit and talk. Lots of "important looking" people are in there chatting. At one point Jeff Ament enters. He talks to one group for a long time. I sat in that room for what felt like forever.... talking to my brother's friend and the sound guy. Chris was nowhere to be seen, nor any other member of the band except Jeff.

On my excitement to head backstage I forgot my bag with my TOTD t-shirt. I mention this to a guy sitting with us. Turns out he is the sound guy for the band. He asks if I want to find it. I say sure and we head into the hall. As I round the corner I spot Chris walking towards me. We see each other and he greets me by name in a low, sleepy voice. "Hey Emily." Jaw drops.... "Uh, hey, Chris..."

My view widens and I spot C-Dog... Chris Jr. He's about as tall as I am. I say hi and notice his full, red lips. Definitely inherited from his Papa! My view widens still and I notice Chris's two lovely daughters. I wave. I look ahead and see his mother in law, Toni chatting away to someone I cannot see. My gaze pans to the right and I see Vicky, putting on a sweater with a red, ruffled v-neck. She's tall, lanky and more beautiful than she appears in photographs. I say hi. She responds with something like "No one ever says HI to me..." And chuckles.

(*note: the rest of this is written AFTER May 18th – June 8th)

"Don't act like a fan..." keeps running through my head. I seem frozen in time. *Too many beers. Too much fandom...* Then Chris comes over to talk to sound guy... Chris is RIGHT IN FRONT OF ME! He and sound guy are talking extensively about how great the show was. Chris seemed pleased.

I recollect now in bits and pieces. I remember thinking "Damn, he's tall. Damn, he's so thin." He wore all black with a jacket and a man bun. I remember stumbling over my words, telling him (casually) that I was heading to find my shirt I left behind in the seats. He nodded gently. I'm not sure he ever quite knew what to say to his admirers. Not sure how long we chatted, but then Chris had to go... and I walked forward to a big curtain with sound guy and asked a bulky security dude if he found a missing shirt. Of course he said no... so back to the small room we went. By the time we turned around to head back to the small room Chris and family were gone.

Inside the room, I remember texting a couple of people about that incredible moment. I told them Chris SAID MY NAME. He remembered me... after I had met him four months before. Who knows, he was probably wondering what the hell I was doing down there.

Shortly after I left the small room, and headed back out alone onto the streets of New York City... to reunite with my friends and recollect my amazing experience. We talked into the wee hours of the night about Chris and company, but mostly about Chris; about how we were drawn to him. How we had followed him around listening to his voice and how much he meant to us. Little did I know that was the last time I'd "see" him.

It was so nice spending time with people who "get it."

It was so nice being a part of music history.

It was so nice that you knew my name.

I will never forget yours.

As you always told us... Thank you, Chris. A million times over. Thank you.

Alone

Seven days have passed since I've seen you last;
Not in person, but on the computer screen.
You seemed so happy.
Your guitar strapped on
And you're in song.
My heart pounds knowing I'll see you up-close again
Soon.

Then the news comes in texts…
I check my phone.
"Are you ok, buddy?"
What??

Another.
"Sorry about Chris. I know he was your favorite."
**

And I know you are gone.
Falling to my knees feels like it takes 27 years
5 months
13 days
16 hours
24 minutes
20 seconds……(and counting)
…. as long as I've loved your voice.

THIS CANNOT BE TRUE because there IS no "end date" to you,
my Dark Knight, Chris.

To be yourself is all that you can do, you sang.
And you helped me do just THAT.

If love could have saved you, mine would have.

*Your funeral took place in L.A. without me, your biggest fan,
And now all I can do is*

isolate …. And

self-medicate

to eradicate my pain.

Now I'm walking like a stone alone.

Emily Wagner

Eric Esrailian

My big brother, Chris Cornell. World needs to know what a loving father, husband, and friend you are - my heart is broken... Say hello to heaven.

Erin McElroy

I wanted to share a memory of Chris and a moment that will be with me forever. It was July 30, 2014. Only a couple of months earlier I was in an auto accident. Hit head on by a distracted driver. My body was still recovering. I was broken both physically and mentally. I was suffering from PTSD, depression and severe anxiety. This, on top of all my physical ailments. Previous to the accident I purchased Soundgarden tickets for me and my husband, Jay. We were beyond excited as they had been a favorite since they began (when we were just barely teenagers). This would be our first time seeing them live!

Now with all my health issues I didn't know how I could go. I was afraid of being in a car, afraid of getting knocked into at the show, afraid to be around all those people. I was simply terrified at the thought. BUT How could I not go??? It's SOUNDGARDEN! How could I deprive my husband of seeing his band? How could I miss this??? I couldn't. So I gathered up all my courage and we set out for the three-hour drive. I was so afraid of being in a car again. I had multiple panic attacks. The only thing keeping me sane was their CDs we brought.

Finally, we made it. I was so broken it felt like it took an eternity to get to my seat. My heart was racing and every inch of my body hurt. I kept thinking that I should be home resting. I was getting angry with the situation. Concerts have always been our thing since we met 20+ years ago. I was angry that a distracted driver could not only flip my life upside down but take away a happy, fun moment from us. I was on the verge of tears...

Then it happened. They walked out, and ahhh what a beautiful sight. Soundgarden was there in the same room as me!! They started playing and it all went away. The air changed. The weight started to lift and all my fears just disappeared. I got so lost in the music. The whole band was brilliant but Chris was such a powerhouse. His voice was so intense. He would hit those high notes. Jay and I would just look at each other and say "HOLY SHIT!!!" He made the hair on the back of our necks stand up. Goosebumps all over. Shivers down our spine. "Beyond the Wheel" and "Jesus Christ Pose" = Blown the fuck away!!!! It was incredible. I can't express the magnitude of emotions I was feeling. Pure euphoria. Pure magic. It was the therapy I needed. What we both needed.

"Fell on Black Days" has particular meaning to me and hearing it live there. There's just no words...

Chris's lyrics have always given me comfort but in this moment he touched my soul in a way I can NEVER put into words. He gave me strength to carry on this journey and to fight through all my struggles. I can't believe he is gone. It's tearing me apart inside. But still I remain grateful. His music and memory will live on in all of us.

RIP Beautiful soul. No one sings like you anymore...

Eva Puma

Fantastic Negrito
(Xavier Dphrepaulezz)

I am at a loss right now.
I have lost a friend.
I love you brother!!!
Life is fragile.
I learned so much from Chris Cornell, watching him perform up close.
The first day I heard Chris Cornell was looking for an opening act I thought there was no way it would work but he is much smarter than me.
He believed in me more than I believed in myself.
He would always come backstage and check on me. Never acted like a BIG celebrity.
I would watch Chris stand in front of a 2k sitting crowd and deliver. I learned watching him.
Another day goes by.
We all will wake tomorrow and press refresh.
Be at peace people of the world.
There is something new happening all the time keep the faith.
Say a prayer for our brother may he find peace finally.

Thank you very much for sharing your thoughts and feelings. I am honored and blessed to know you all through Chris!!

The fans of Chris Cornell are so full of thank you for so much sharing and supporting!!

We wake today better because our brother Chris Cornell touched our lives and left us with the gift of his music and his profound kindness.

I am sitting in my car and I am laughing at a great Chris memory.

Chris got a kick out of what I wore. It amused him! He would say: "wait a minute you're wearing a necktie and a neck scarf."

He would have a big smile and try to adjust my scarf, lol. I was always glad that it amused him.

I'm sitting here a little choked up. He was a good man, a good person, he always asked about my family. He never asked for anything.

I am very, very blessed and fortunate to have crossed paths with such a genuine human being.

I remember during the Temple Of The Dog tour Chris stopped the sound check just to meet my son.

This life we live. We don't have to be happy all the time

My heart hurts, my face smiles.

Hi Chris!!

People loved you! They still love you.

My eyes water my throat tightens, good memories keep me fightin'.

I'm good. Hanging in the donut shop I used to play in front of before Chris gave me a job.

Chris opening statement to me was: "I'm gonna introduce you to my audience man." I was terrified, lol.

This life is mostly good.

If you are feeling desperate or isolated reach out to a friend.

Photo: Doc Thomas

Gaby Nieva

With His Own Words

I don't want this sadness go away
Because it'll mean that I will lose you for good.

I was born with a broken heart
With your voice always present in my life.
Reminding me that I should try to live every day,
Going hungry for better times...
Even in a world full of dead.

But the pain is always there
Like a constant reminder
Of all the things, the sacred things,
that I lost in the way.

Say hello 2 heaven for me Chris
Cause my path, I believe, is not over yet.

THANK YOU: A TRIBUTE TO CHRIS CORNELL

Although you go home too early
No one will ever could sing to my soul like you did it.

I never really wanted to stay here for a long time
But my call I think I still don't receive
And yet my road will be as dark as your black days I'm afraid,
Now that your verse is incomplete and without a tune.

The pain is always screaming, and it will always be.
I was on my knees so many times
Feeling like Minnesota but never ever wanted to look like California.
And yet, in a way or another,
I will always find it how to get on my feet again.

So now it is time to say thank you my friend
Your words light my life
And your tune guide my heart.
Thank you for borrow me your lyrics
And making my way easier to walk.
I am not using your words as mine,
But as an example of how they have always been with me.

Forever, through the ages, thank you.

Gaby Nieva, from México

Gaia Cornell

You will always be my sweet sunshower. The only thing I can say is: Thank you. For helping me in the worst days of my life and for giving me the happiest moments during your concerts. You are part of my heart and my soul and it will be forever.

THANK YOU: A TRIBUTE TO CHRIS CORNELL

Photo: Dawn Belotti

With Soundgarden, Webster Hall, June 2, 2014.

Galaxy Starr

For Chris

Soundgarden
Although we never met face to face, you know me.
You sing my youth. Your carnal scream shapes my years.
Your words give my emotions a sound; the cosmic vibration that IS your voice.
Temple of the Dog
Although we never met face to face, you know me.
You sing his death. Your soulful scream pierces my ears.
Your words go through my broken soul; the universe understands.
Audioslave
Although we never met face to face, you know me.
You sing my life.
Your ferocious scream breaks my fears.
Your words challenge my thoughts; the infinite possibilities.
Silence
Although we never met face to face, you knew me.

THANK YOU: A TRIBUTE TO CHRIS CORNELL

You sing no more.
Your angelic voice now ushers my tears.
Your music haunts my dreams; the melancholy nights.
My Voice
Although we never met face to face, you knew me.
I sing for you.
My shaky voice testifies for you here.
Your existence enriched the world; you are beautiful eternity.

Dedicated to Chris Cornell - Rest Easy Sweet Soul. You are missed, loved and will always be remembered. Thank you for your gift to the word.

Galaxy Starr 6/18/17 5:47am

Giles Kristian

As an artist you inspired me. Your music and your voice lifted and transported me. In more recent times we became friends and you gave me kind and wise words of comfort when my father passed. I'm glad I was able to thank you in some small way. I'll miss you but you will inspire me still, and you live on in your music and your family and those of us whose lives you touched. Farewell, Chris.

Gina DiNolfi McMillen

Here's one of my favorite treasures from the reunion show. They opened with "Gun". It was amazing.

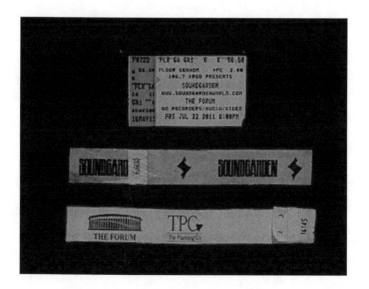

Glad Ruiz

Chris will always be a part of my heart.

He taught me that it's OK to feel your dark feelings and they do have a place in your life.

Greta Kennedy

I've been a huge Soundgarden fan since the 90's, and Chris and Layne were who I considered my rockstar husbands :)

I was so excited to hear that Soundgarden was coming back to tour in 2017 and that they were coming to Atlanta (where I live) so of course I had to be there! I saw that they were playing on my birthday in Detroit (where I grew up) so I thought it was the perfect way to celebrate and called up a friend I had not seen in almost 10 years. We sat on our phones and laptops as soon as tickets went on sale trying to get the best seats! We ended up about 5th row on the floor for the sold out show at the Fox.

It was the perfect way to spend my birthday! The crowd and energy was amazing! The band played a great set list and Chris nailed it!

I woke up the next morning to my phone bombarded with missed calls and texts, and I was thinking it was friends who I had not spoken with the day before, calling to wish me a belated birthday. When I saw what happened, it wasn't real. I was in shock and so upset because he seemed so excited to be performing for all of his fans just hours before. I'm still in disbelief over what happened, but I'm glad I got to see his last show and to see all the love and appreciation his fans had for him that night and will continue to have for him!

THANK YOU: A TRIBUTE TO CHRIS CORNELL

Heather N.E. Jones

Chris, I'm still having a hard time comprehending that you are no longer here with us. My heart is broken for your family, friends and fans. It's unbelievable how this has affected so many around the world. I believe we all are finding comfort in sharing our experiences about you and your music.

You spoke to us with your poetic lyrics, and you sang to us from your soul. I did not know you personally, but some how it felt like I did. I hope you knew how much you meant to the world. We miss you already.

As a fan of yours since I was 15 years old, I listen to you daily. I heard someone recently say your music was a soundtrack to their youth. To me your music is a soundtrack to my life. It always seemed like you read a page from my book and wrote a song about them.

I got to thank you once, you smiled and nodded. I was blessed to hear you live several times. Your voice was so powerful and seemed surreal. Thank you for the music. Truly no one sings like you anymore. I know you are singing with the angels now.

Heather N.E. Jones (CCFAN_HNE)

THANK YOU: A TRIBUTE TO CHRIS CORNELL

Holly Curtis

Chris, you helped me through my darkest times with your lyrical poetry... too many times. I never met you, yet your beautiful soul touched my life in so many ways there isn't enough time to write it all. You were and still remain an inspiration to me, and millions of others. I can't thank you enough, but every time I sing, you are on my mind and always within my heart and soul.... Music is infinite.... Love you Chris.

Ingrid Crane

He was our best friend and didn't know it. The tragedy of this is beyond comprehension. But let's use this to create and be the best that we can be. He'd want us to. Let's do something.

Ivonne Caro

Chris, where do I start? Do I go as far back as 1988/1989 when I first heard Soundgarden? Or back to February 3, 1990 in Tampa, Florida, two days shy of 19, when you pulled me out of a mosh pit, put me on a chair, got me ice for my bloody lip and nose and kept the ice on my face until it was numb? You then made a comment about us having identical hair. Lol. It was the first time I saw Soundgarden play and the first time we met. That was the moment I became a fan of Chris Cornell, the man.

On 22nd August 1992, backstage, at Lollapalooza in Miami, I was speechless when you remembered me, and my less than stellar first impression. Countless shows and meet and greets and you were always kind, generous and humble.

Never once did I say, "thank you", for the gift of your talent and the person you were. It's killing me inside. I took it for granted. I thought you were eternal. I never got to thank you for getting me through the darkest periods and places in my life. I never told you that it has been your lyrics/poetry that I recite over and over, in my head, when I'm doing my cancer treatments, when I'm at a low point mentally, and when I am sick as a dog from side effects. I'm so remorseful for not saying thank you, when I was given the chance.

So to Vicky and the kids, I will express my eternal gratitude for sharing you with us and being so gracious. Rest In Peace, Chris, and thank you.

With eternal gratitude, Ivonne Caro (née Rivera).

Jacqueline S.

For Chris Cornell.

Tomorrow is going to be a tough day. Tomorrow is Chris Cornell's funeral, and I'm not ready to let him go.

It's Thursday evening and I'm sitting staring at my screen, this is something that I never wanted to write. It has taken time to gather my thoughts, but I need to say this.

Last Thursday I woke up to texts and messages, and as I read them my first thought was please God don't let this be true, but as I read more I felt sick, then shocked, devastated and numb, it was true, our beloved Chris was gone.

I know that some people will not understand, they'll say I'm crazy for mourning someone I never met or knew, that there are terrible things happening in the world, why don't I feel for them, but that's not how it works. There are many, many others out there who will understand, and so I hope you don't mind me sharing my feelings with you.

He believed in speaking from the heart, so this is what I will try to do, although words can never fully express how I feel.

Occasionally I'm angry at the universe, this wasn't supposed to happen, he was supposed to be here for the rest of my life, or another 30 years at least, writing and playing his brilliant words and music and enjoying his life and family. If I'm honest, a small part of me still refuses to believe that his incredible, powerful voice has been silenced. It has got to be a horrible mistake, surely? He has been an important part of my life for over two decades, a bright burning light; today the world feels colder and darker.

It all started in the early 90s, when I was in my early 20s. I was walking back to work from lunch when this sound hit me, coming from a radio playing in a shop I was passing, it was Nirvana's "Smells Like Teen Spirit". I stopped on the spot and listened, there was something about it that I instantly loved. Later, when I got home, I was determined to find out all about this band and any other bands that were part of this new, for me, music scene coming out of Seattle. The next band I discovered was Soundgarden.

At first, it wasn't the music or lyrics that caught my attention, it was his voice. There has been so much written about Chris Cornell's voice by people far more eloquent than I am, so all I can do is say what it meant, and still means, to me. It soared, it reached me in a way no other voice had, I felt like it touched my soul. It's now 25 years later, and he's been with me ever since. When I have a good day, I play his music loud and bounce round the house, when my day is bad his words and music are there for me, he understands, and when I'm lost he lights my way home. It is a voice that can perfectly express love and passion, rage and pain, it is raw and pure and there will never be another like it.

I've always been what I'd call a quiet fan. I've never had a large, active presence online or in the fan community, and I'm not one of the wonderfully talented people who can create works of art or design websites, I've just been there in the background all this time, loving every song, every album, reading/listening to/watching every interview and seeing him play live whenever I could. I guess there are a lot of fans like me, and he knew we were there. I hope that all of you who have been more active will forgive me for suddenly appearing now and reaching out to you.

I feel privileged that I was able to see him play live seven times. That doesn't seem enough now, but I always thought I'd have more time. I know that I'm lucky, as there will be many who were not able to see him this often.

I have so many great, and some funny, memories from his gigs, so I'll share a few. At an Audioslave gig at Brixton Academy, I was rescued by a very friendly, very large tattooed man when the moshing expanded rapidly in my direction during "Killing in the Name". I'm not very tall, I would have been squished!

Standing at the front near a speaker at the Camden Roundhouse, he hit such an extraordinary note I was deaf in one ear for three days, but it was worth it.

At the London Palladium, his performance of "When I'm Down" was everything, it sent shivers down my spine, and he made up a song about Transylvania on the spot that was clever and funny and made me laugh.

The last time I saw him was at the incredible concert in The Royal Albert Hall. His amalgamation of U2 and Metallica was brilliant and his version of "Nothing Compares 2 U" made me cry (and always will do.) Above all, I remember his electric presence and the sound of his strong, beautiful voice live. I'm having trouble coming to terms with the fact that I won't hear it again.

What else did I love about him? Among many things, his smile and his humour, his intelligence and the eloquence that marked his lyrics and interviews, his gentleness and the fact that he cared and wanted to do some good in the world.

It is said that time heals, and that's ok if you've got a broken leg, but not so much with grief. In recent years I've lost my father and other loved ones and in my experience (although everyone's experience is different) you don't "get over it". At first grief and pain seems overwhelming, and then it hits in waves. This will never be ok. Pain like this never truly goes away, time just allows it to become less sharp, less intrusive so that you can live with it, it becomes a part of you.

So here I am, near the end of my writing. What do we do

now? Well, first we allow ourselves to take the time we need to mourn, and we talk. Talking is important. This is difficult for me as I'm not good at talking about anything that deeply affects me, which is why I've put this in writing; do whatever helps you. We share our memories, we celebrate his life, we keep listening to his music and we never forget.

I won't say goodbye, as his words and music will always be with me, so instead I will say farewell. Farewell my brilliant, gentle, soulful, passionate and complicated Chris. You made the world a better place by being in it and you made a difference to me. I will miss you so very much.

Jacqueline S.

Jade Bars

My Dearest CC, I so miss your presence in this world. Your natural charisma when in front of an audience. Your loving gaze when you sneaked secret glances at your wife - it was beautiful to see such a genuine love. Your intoxicating voice which has never failed to cull any of my storms and draw me out of the dark. Your demeanour, just so refreshingly authentic. No pretense. The fame never went to your head.

It is so difficult to accept your death and I will ache for you, for your family, for your friends, for your fans for months to come, if not years. As if you weren't gorgeous enough to look at, it was your humility that made you beautiful. You had a beautiful soul and maybe it's the loss of someone so genuine, so authentic, so humble that leaves this world with such a void.

I thank you for sharing your gift with the world. You met me many times in my darkness, unbeknownst to you of course. And while I still have all the same albums, this will never mitigate the sense of loss I, and the rock community, feels. One day my graces will flower in a sweet sunshower, but that sun will forever be a black hole sun.

Rest peacefully CC

With love, appreciation, and admiration, Jade.

Jade Fish

Chris, since the day you left us, my heart has been shattered into a million pieces. I started listening to your band, Soundgarden, at ten years old. It was the music that I would first call all my own. As I grew into my teenage years, your music grew as well. Audioslave became a favorite band, and Soundgarden remained my all time favorite. Then as I grew into adulthood, your solo and acoustic songs became the soundtrack to my 20's and 30's.

I will forever hold a place in my heart for you. Sleep well and I'll see you when I get to where you are.

Jade Fish.

Jamal Sampson

I never met Chris Cornell, but all of his music kept me SO, SO happy inside. He will FOREVER be missed.

James Benger

Goodnight

In 1990, when I was eight-years-old,
I sat on my thirteen-year-old cousin's waterbed
as he played me a tape he called *Ultramega OK*.
I remember being so blown away
by the guitars,
the bass,
the drums,
but mostly that voice,
those words.
I was transported somewhere else,
somewhere I was bigger,
simply more
than my years allowed,
but still me.

Four years later,
the same cousin gave me

a somewhat used *Superunknown* t-shirt
and a tape called *Badmotorfinger*.
and my childhood,
my adolescence was defined.

Last night you stopped breathing.

I could tell you how much you've meant to me,
how I studied your lyrics and your fingers,
how I played your albums for my son
when he was only two-months-old.

I could tell you how angry I am with you,
how distraught,
how I've spent all day on the verge of tears.

How you changed my life,
how I admired how you kept it together,
how you took care of your family
despite it all.

How I'm going to miss you for a long time,
probably forever.

We never met,
but I knew your records inside out.
You were like the distant older brother
I never had.

I listened to your records all day today,
trying so hard to find some new meaning,
but all I found was the same elation

THANK YOU: A TRIBUTE TO CHRIS CORNELL

mixed with a new tinge of seeping wound.

Tonight I will close my eyes and
listen to *Songbook*,
and your voice will put me to sleep,
just like all those years ago,
and that will have to be enough,
because now that's all we'll ever have.

I don't know where you are,
or even if you are,
but I hope you found it;
whatever it was you were
searching so long to get,
whatever it was that
none of us could give you,
I hope you found it.
I hope you're happy.
I hope you're finally resting.

Goodnight, Sir,
goodnight.

James Howton

I woke the same, as any other day, except a voice told me news that I'm still reeling over. Jennifer said: "Baby, I have some news, and it's not good." I was half asleep still so I braced myself. She told me that Chris Cornell had passed. I immediately said: "No, that can't be right." I knew she wasn't kidding. To do so in our house wouldn't be right.

We just saw Soundgarden less than two weeks ago. He was on top of his craft like he always was. To be even talking about him in the past tense just seems wrong. It is wrong. I always imagined him being this guy who would be on a stage somewhere until he was old.

I fell in love with Soundgarden in junior high before they were well known. They, with all the other Seattle bands were part of my soundtrack to life. They helped me through those awkward adolescent years and continued to inspire me throughout my adult life.

Chris could scream like a banshee one minute then croon like a soul singer the next. No one could and never will match his range or style. He was truly one of a kind. He inspired many singers and bands. The kinship he had with Eddie Vedder and all the guys from Pearl Jam was a brotherhood. To his brothers in Soundgarden I know this is incredibly heart wrenching. To his wife and kids I can't imagine the loss. He once wrote a line for Andy Wood that was "I never wanted to write these words down for you". That's how I'm feeling right now. I can't believe I'm writing this about one of my heroes. It's surreal, and I can't completely wrap my brain around it. He had so much to live for.

We had the pleasure of seeing Soundgarden twice and Chris on his solo acoustic tour in the last three years. One of my favorite concert memories was seeing Chris at the Ryman Theater in Nashville on my 40th birthday. It was a beautiful, intimate show that I will never forget. In it he professed his love for his wife. How she inspired him.

Also, Soundgarden has been working on an album. So I think he had too much to live for. I just refuse to think his death was a clear-cut suicide. I've wondered for a while if he may have been sick. It's just a weird feeling I've had. Maybe I'm just trying to make it easier in my own head.

No matter what, he is gone. I'm in tears as I write this. A grown man. That's how much I love music. It's personal for me. I feel like I've lost a family member. Although I never met him, it's still like I knew him through the great music he left as his legacy. That's the power of song, I say it all the time. For people who don't get it, they never will. For those of us who do, it's an unspoken fact of life.

I'll close by saying 'Thank You' Chris Cornell. Thank you for baring your soul to the world. Thank you for inspiring me to write early in my teenage years and still to this day. Thank you for giving me and my wife those great concert experiences of which I'll forever treasure.

Rest easy, sing with the angels, and "Say Hello To Heaven".

Janet Hall

Your voice, indescribable.
Your music and lyrics, like poetry.
A genius and beautiful inside & out.
Thank you for everything you've done for your fans.
You helped a lot of people through your music and the many ways that you gave to the world.
The world and music will never be the same without you.
Rest in peace. Gone too soon, you will not be forgotten.

THANK YOU: A TRIBUTE TO CHRIS CORNELL

Janine Munson

The year was 1991. I was a new mom with my son, Ian, and was lucky enough to be able to be home with him 24/7. I loved metal and many other genres of music. Metal has always been my #1 favorite. I heard the first chords of "Outshined" and said: "WOW!! These guys sound like the next Led Zeppelin!" Yes, I said it exactly like that. I was so stoked to hear some amazing sound coming out of my stereo. That is my story. There is a LOT more to it. But, that is how it all started.

Let me add, I brought my Ian to a Chris Cornell show and that is when my EXTREMELY talented guitar-playing son realized he wanted to play in front of an audience. CC was a powerful performer. Thanks for listening. #LoudLove

Photo: Dawn Belotti

With Soundgarden, Terminal 5. January 16, 2013.

Jared Schmidt

Like so many others, I was simply moved by Soundgarden from the very first time I ever heard them. That helped forge a very strong passion not only listening to music, but it helped my find my creative voice as well. That will never leave me, and it all started with Chris's songs.

THANK YOU: A TRIBUTE TO CHRIS CORNELL

Jason C. Geer

Simply, the sweetest euphoria, the raw emotion and passion in his voice. Blessed to have heard him live.

THANK YOU: A TRIBUTE TO CHRIS CORNELL

Photo: Dawn Belotti

With Soundgarden, Webster Hall, 2 June 2014.

Jay Cee Lopez

I met Chris Cornell in Miami, Florida on my birthday, 29th October 2015. I was able to chat with him for about 15 minutes at the meet and greet. He was the sweetest most gentle artist I ever met and I have met quiet a few.

CC's music has helped get over low moments in my life, break-ups, etc. We chatted about music and his foundation with Vicky, which he was very passionate about. I was trying to remain calm and avoid acting like a fan boy in front of him, but I was able to tell him that my favorite song was "Blow Up The Outside World" due to its lyrical content, which I was able to relate with.

I was so overwhelmed with him signing my memorabilia and taking pics that I forgot to tell him that it was my birthday. Needless to say it was already one of my best memorable birthdays ever, but it would only get better. The show began and everyone at the venue was in awe and admiration, the crowd kept on giving him a standing ovation after almost every song. Chris is well known to talk to the audience during his solo shows, and today was not the exception as he began to introduce the next song he told a brief story which made my night. Quoting Chris, "Earlier tonight I met a fan and this is his favorite song" as he began strumming the guitar to the chords of "Blow Up The Outside World". Unforgettable moment for me as a long time CC fan.

Jeff Anderson

When I was a young teenager, I had a lot of issues with depression and major anxiety, personal demons. I had always been into music in some form or another, but I had gotten away from much of the music I had earlier listened to, and really at that point, had not had much of anything to help me through my own personal struggles as a kid.

I lived across the street from a public swimming pool, and spent a lot of my time there. They had a large P.A. system in place and played a lot of rock radio over the summer. It was there I first heard "Black Hole Sun" in 1994. I took a liking to that song immediately but thought nothing much of it until my mother approached me about her Columbia House membership. She needed one more album to complete her order, and wanted to know if there was anything I wanted. I didn't have much at the time I wanted but I told her I liked that Soundgarden song, so I'll take that *Superunknown* album.

I remember the day it came. I was home, sick from school, so I put it in my player and listened to it. From that day forward my life was different. That album intrigued me on so many levels, it was so different from anything I had heard at that point in my life. From the intensity and complex musical composition, to the ethereal quality of the arrangements, screaming yet subtle guitar tracks, low melodic bass lines, superbly crafted drumming and through it all, the most amazing, powerful, elegant yet fierce voice I had ever heard. The band was amazing, their music and lyrics were incredible. And Chris Cornell had me hooked forever with his voice.

I quickly saved my money to get my hands on anything and everything Soundgarden and Chris Cornell related. I found a copy of the original *Screaming Life/ Fopp* EP, and soon after a cassette of the Temple Of The Dog album. Which is one of, if not the most brilliant piece of music I've ever listened to. And when I passed my first degree black belt test, my mom purchased *Badmotorfinger* for me as a gift. I listened to all those cassettes until they literally fell apart. It was that one song at a public pool, and a random chance ordering of an album, that set the course of my own musical course, as a musician, in motion.

I soon after met a man that agreed to purchase me a brand new guitar, on the grounds I work in his yard that summer to pay it off. I quickly agreed and soon began my quest for other people to play with. Over the years, my tastes in music varied to many different levels and grew much heavier, and with the multitude of bands I myself played with, I used my influences I had drawn on to practice my craft. Through it all, Chris Cornell was my number one influence, and every project he immersed himself in, became my study.

He never put himself into anything I didn't like, and I believe everything he touched turned to gold musically. He was an elegant songwriter, with lyrics that captured your imagination and soul, with a voice that could be the smoothest, coolest croon, to the shrieking wail of Hell's deepest hole. He was brilliance encapsulated in a man, that was as enigmatic and mysterious as was his music.

I have played in many bands over the years, been a part of a lot of neat things, toured some, and enjoyed most of my life with music. And I owe all of it to him, a man I never met, yet felt I knew so well... as he was such a part of my life through ups and downs and good and bad... He was a constant pillar.

Until that night in May.

I'm still in shock and mourning as I know millions of people like me are as well. My heart goes out to his family and friends. They lost a father, brother, husband, son... the world lost am amazing man, talent, musician and inspiration. I often daydreamed over the years, that if I ever got to be famous or popular as a musician, and they interviewed me, asking who were my influences and who did I love most... I always dreamed of saying all of the bands and musicians that were important to me, but finishing with Chris Cornell and Soundgarden... as they were the cornerstone in my musical path, and in some respects, life itself. They defined an era for me, and influenced me like no one else ever has, or likely ever will. And they will always be my favorite.

I often dreamed of this scenario, thinking, maybe by chance, when I say this to the magazine, or interviewer, maybe by some chance Chris will read it, or hear it... maybe he will see it somehow, and he will know, what he meant to me as a person, as a musician... And maybe some day, I will be at a party, or show, and he will be there... and maybe I will get the chance to introduce myself, and he will have seen what I had said, and I would get the privilege of meeting with him, and most of all, the chance to tell him thank you... Thank you for all the sleepless nights your music helped make bearable... Thank you for all the times when I was too down or beat up to take another step, your voice picked me back up... Thank you for all the times when I wanted to give up, but your inspiration brought me back to my work... Thank you for all your lyrics that I always identified with, no matter my mood... You always said something that for the time... and thank you for sharing your gifts with us... the millions and millions that you never knew, that you performed for and gave your life's energy to enjoy.... Thank you for helping me be me... I only wish I could have done the same for you...

But this was only a dream, and now that day will never come. A dream I've had many times over the years... I am not a famous musician... I still work 70 hours a week to raise a family... I still write and play music and perform when I can. But the dream still existed... the possibility... I still try... It could still happen... or at least it could have... until that night... At least part of that dream ended, as no matter what may come, I will never get the chance to thank you for all those things and tell you what you meant to me, a nobody that you helped in so many ways...

So, I will take this opportunity to tell you it all here, as unfortunate as it is, and I hope somewhere, somehow, maybe in the superunknown, you can see this or hear this... Thank you and I love you man. Rest in peace.

Jenifer Farmer

Dear Chris: You saved my life!! I know many have said this about your heartfelt poetry, turned to song. I was always aware of Soundgarden, not crazy into them, like some, but aware of this powerhouse of a voice fronting them. Years later (early 2000's), I was in a very dark place, having been betrayed by someone I thought loved me as much as I did him. I had decided to end it by my own hand. Bathtub full of water (I did not want anyone to have to clean up my mess), razor blade on the tub rim, radio blaring to my favorite rock station. As I lay there in the water, crying, I see the full moon come into sight in the skylight, just as the radio played "Like A Stone" and then "Sunshower" back to back (a twofer, as they called it!). It was like you were speaking to me personally not to go through with it, that everything would be ok! I have loved you ever since.

    I think that's why your death hurts so bad, because you were my age, and because you touched so many with your words and music. I am so, so sorry, Chris, that no one was there for you in your darkest hour, that you couldn't hold on for one more day when things may have looked better. I will love you and listen to your music forever.

    Loud Love Brother, Jen Farmer.

Jenni Hollister

Thank you for the music...
You'll be so missed and you were so loved... May your music live and rock on forever xxx RIP Chris...
With love... Jenni, Sydney, Australia.

Jennifer D. Burke

When I first became aware of Chris Cornell in the early 90s, I was instantly mesmerized by his presence and voice. I had never seen or heard an artist like him before. What started out as a silly teenage crush, soon turned into a lifetime of admiration. Whatever I was experiencing, his music was always my escape. Lyrically, I believe he was one of the most prolific and sincere.

On May 18th, I felt like I lost a friend. I didn't understand why I was so deeply affected and then realized it was because he shared so much of his own life, the darkness he often faced, through his music. He connected with us.

I feel truly blessed and honored that I had the opportunity to see him perform live in the recent years. He leaves behind an incredible legacy that influenced not only my life, but an entire generation. I will forever listen to his music that I love so much but now it comes with a heavy heart.

Rest peacefully, Chris. Thank you for making this world a better place.

- Jennifer D. Burke

THANK YOU: A TRIBUTE TO CHRIS CORNELL

Jennifer Wallace

I needed a little time to gather my thoughts, though it is still hard to believe. The world has lost a legend, a one of a kind rock god. Such a tragic loss. As a long-time fan, naturally I'm upset. But my heart aches for his family, wife and children.

I was lucky enough to see him in concert solo/acoustic, with Soundgarden and Audioslave at least five times. One of those times was at a smaller venue. I was able to make my way to the front of the stage. It was surreal.

To give you an idea of the type of man he was, this past Mother's Day he tweeted to his mother in law "Thank you for creating the love of my life."

Obviously, I didn't know him personally, but from what I've gathered he was a sensitive, gentle soul with a soft heart. It tends to be these types of people who suffer the most. Lots of speculation around what actually happened in that hotel room, but it's somewhat irrelevant. The amount of pain his wife must be in is unimaginable. In the blink of an eye, her entire world came crashing down. I have no idea how she's going to cope with such a devastating loss. Heartbroken for her.

His incredible voice and lyrics will live on and touch many generations to come. I suppose now all we can do is be grateful that he shared his gift with all of us. RIP beautiful man.

Jerry D. Traurig

What I have is very little. The only time I saw Soundgarden in concert was in '94, in Milwaukee, and Milwaukee is known for beer brewing companies. Chris said "what's everyone drinking, Budweiser? I drink piss." It got quiet. I thought it was weird coming from him, funny yet awkward, that's all.

Jill Haley

Chris helps us say fuck cancer in honor of Rose Hurt's recovery.

Joanne Roughsedge

My moment with Chris... at a show in San Diego I was standing outside the back door of the venue talking to the 70ish security guard. I see Chris walk by... so this is how it went in my mind, I gently move the gentleman aside and slowly walk up to him. What my husband said happened was... I threw the man to the ground, leapt over him and ran screaming, arms flailing yelling "CHRIS!!!!!!!!"

I think the real story is in the middle somewhere. Oh and he looked at me like a crazy woman (probably 45 at the time) and walked through the door.

It was another amazing show.

BY THE FANS AND FRIENDS OF CHRIS CORNELL

Photos: Joanne Roughsedge

Jodi Smith

Why doesn't anyone believe in loneliness? Compassion is a science. No one likes to talk about loneliness or suicide. They go hand in hand. Hopefully, with Chris's passing this subject will be addressed more.

To me Chris was more Jesus-like than Jesus.

Joe Broussard IV

So, almost two years ago my oldest son, who was only two at the time, was diagnosed with a chronic kidney disease. A few months after that, I lost my job. With tens of thousands of dollars in medical bills, and no income, we were in a terrible place financially. In order to avoid losing our home, we rented it out and moved in to my mother in law's basement. With two little boys, one with a chronic disease, a growing mountain of debt, and no job, there were days that I didn't want to get out of bed.

One thing that helped me to keep moving forward was the song "Rowing". I would listen to it, and cry helplessly, and scream along, and borrow strength. This song helps keep me moving forward for my family.

One night, years ago, when my wife and I were still dating, we were at a bar and the DJ was taking requests. I was feeling pretty loose, and requested this song ["The Curse" by Audioslave], then I took her to the dance floor and proceeded to scream along (I know you do it too) as if I were alone in my car. She was so taken by my passion that she declared this "our song." Eventually, it was our first dance at our wedding. I was really just trying to drunkenly channel Chris. . . But this is a happy song for me.

Photo: Pixabay

John Barbara

Dance with Mortality.

I loved the intensity of your music… the soaring heights of your voice. I was mesmerized by your mischievous smile… that halo of hair… your eyes… your swagger. Maybe I didn't realize how much I cared until I heard about your death. The news hit like a punch in the gut and I'm reeling with disbelief at the depth of my sadness. Maybe in some ways, this grief I feel is a cathartic release for all the angst, pain, emotion and relief tied to my own dance with mortality. Maybe when I see you again, I will tell you that I understood. Maybe then, we will both be at peace.

John Eric Osborn

I've been a teacher for about seven years now... I teach art. I often (almost every day) play music for my students, ages ranging from 11-14. Guess what music we heard in my class all the time? Anyway, today was the first time since his death that I didn't come home sobbing like a big sissy. The kids, some of them anyway, were kind of touched that I was so moved by his passing. I am glad to say that I played a part in exposing them to quality stuff. I hope that, wherever Chris Cornell is, he saw that he was making new fans every damn day in my class. Artsy rock and roll can live on in the best of 'em, I say.

God Bless y'all.

Joseph Baker

I am a musician and when I was around 11 years old I discovered the Grunge music scene from Seattle, Washington. My favorite band was instantly Soundgarden. The lyrics were dark and beautiful, and the music was heavy and innovative.

In 2017 when I was 13 years old my Mom told me that Soundgarden would be headlining the Beale Street Music Festival in our hometown of Memphis, Tennessee. I could not believe it, it was a dream come true. This was my first music festival ever and it could not have been better. I was right near the stage positioned pretty close to Chris Cornell. My mom and I were just feet from the stage.

The performance was amazing and the band played all of my favorites that night – "Fell on Black Days", "Spoonman", "Rusty Cage", "Black Hole Sun", and "Flower". I got Chris Cornell's setlist after the show.

I was heartbroken when I found out about Chris' death. He is still one of my heroes and I am so lucky to have been able to see him perform. I will remember that concert for the rest of my life.

Thank you, Chris, for being an amazing musician and human being.

Joseph Baker, age 13, Memphis, Tennessee.

THANK YOU: A TRIBUTE TO CHRIS CORNELL

BY THE FANS AND FRIENDS OF CHRIS CORNELL

Photo: Jospeh Baker

Jovelle Baker

I think I've finally figured out why this loss is like no other. For me, I think it's because he was not a typical egotistical celebrity. He was not the epitome of a spoiled rock star.

He was a sensitive, compassionate being that respected his fellow humans whether they were rich, poor, or otherwise.

Let's face it, they don't make 'em like that anymore. He would have been someone that we would have been lucky to know had he just been a guy with a regular job with no fame or fortune.

To me, knowing how big his heart was and how deeply he felt about life and his love for others is probably why the tears just won't stop falling.

This place will never be the same without you, Chris Cornell.

Julie Harris

Where to begin? I started following Chris Cornell on twitter in 2009. I met my bccf (best Chris Cornell friend) Rose. She lives in ND and I live in SD. We instantly connected. She was well intertwined with many others already, from all over the US and other countries. These people welcomed me into their circle.

When Soundgarden announced their reunion tour in 2011, we were all so excited. Talking and planning about which shows we would "meet up" at. Red Rocks in Morrison, CO was where we (my husband and I) met most of these friends. Our kids thought we were crazy to meet up with people we met on the internet. We had a blast!

When I purchased the book *Photophantasm*, my husband about died when I told him how much I'd spent on it. For those who aren't familiar with the book... it is full of stories and pictures of Soundgarden concerts and meetings with fellow "Cornellians". I am so glad I spent the money. I'm thankful to those people who put the time and love into this book. I am thankful for the friendships I still have with those people. I'm thankful you all understand the heartache that I am going through. Normal people don't "get" why I was a snivelling mess for the last three days, plus more to come. I love Chris for bringing these people into my life, I will forever be grateful to him. My heart breaks for his family and for all of you.

Photo: Doc Thomas

Julie McNamara

These pictures were taken at White Rock Beach, in BC Canada. After my daughter and I found out Chris Cornell had died, we were shattered . We went down there with our concert shirts on and just spent the whole day talking about his music his voice and we talked about how lucky we were to go to many of his concerts, like Soundgarden two times, Songbook, and Audioslave.

I'm 48 and have been a Chris Cornell fan since the beginning. My boyfriend's favourite CD before his died in a motorcycle accent was Audioslave. I played "Like a Stone" at his funeral.

Chris Cornell had a way with his voice of soothing your inner soul. He was unique - if you felt energy, serenity, anger, hurt or you wanna dance. He expressed it all and looked beautiful doing it. Thank you Chris Cornell for leaving myself and my daughter the most amazing and magical musical imprint. We miss you we love you always.

Julie and daughter Jessica.

THANK YOU: A TRIBUTE TO CHRIS CORNELL

Julie Timmons

I am approaching 49, so I've been on this earth almost as long as Chris Cornell. His music has been woven into my soul from throughout the span of his long career. Soundgarden, solo, Audioslave and my personal all time favorite album ever, Temple of The Dog, they all invoke memories and can sometimes bring me back to a different time in my life just by hearing a song. The TOTD CD has literally been in the CD player of my car for YEARS.

Out of the MANY concerts and shows I've been to, including Soundgarden and Audioslave, his solo show at the Shubert Theatre in Boston, MA October 2015 was THE BEST EVER. We had front row seats and CC was and always will be my musical idol.

It's so sad to think he won't be making music anymore. I am not one to cry/mourn over a celebrity.
Elvis… nope.
Lennon… nope.
Bowie… nope.
Prince… nope.

I can appreciate their individual impact on music but none

made me really sad.
 Chris Cornell... this one kicked me in the gut.
 RIP CC, you will be missed.

Julio Zaldivar Suarez

Well, I live in Lima, Peru. Fan of Chris and Soundgarden since 1990. SG played here for the first time in 2014 and Chris was here just last December on the Higher Truth acoustic South American tour.

I have a little story to tell.

I inquired with my contacts inside the show production, and knew the band will stay at the Ritz. So, I booked one room for one night to been able to stay inside the hotel facilities and increase my chances to meet them, especially Chris who I knew was very reserved.

Anyway, I was there the time they arrived to the hotel and the ONLY time Chris was showing himself was on the check-in desk of the hotel. I was in a suit, avoided being dressed as a fanboy, so I approached the desk at the same time and said "Hi" very respectfully. Told him I was a long-time fan and I'm just happy with meeting him and a handshake, and that I was thankful to him for making the soundtrack of my life. He smiled and gave me a handshake but before do that he put his hand on his coat pocket, I knew after that was to give me a handful of guitar picks. He also was so gracious to sign a couple of things I put on the desk without asking anything. Of course I didn't ask for a picture as I consider that was too pushy and as his personal bodyguard was giving more attention to the main door and I knew he will notice me any moment...

So, that was it, he was all the time at his room, just went to the soundcheck and to the gig, all the times in a private car and by hotel's car door. So I consider myself lucky met him but it cost me the eternal hate of his bodyguard....well...

In the December acoustic show, he talked to the public and told us he composed "I Am The Highway" in his room in Lima in 2014, so all we was impressed.

When wearing my SG Superunknown tour shirt and carrying my white Maximum Breakage shirt, the one with Kim smiley face on the front and the original SG Name "Louder than fuck" on red letter in the back, I was on the fence and screamed to Kim and show him his smiley pic. He pointed at me, then he pointed me and talks to Chris... then Chris pointed me and talks to Ben... Ben came to Chris' mic and reads my shirt and screamed "LOUDER THAN FUCK!" and that was magical to me...

This is the ticket of the SG show in Lima.

BY THE FANS AND FRIENDS OF CHRIS CORNELL

Here's is the first ever time Chris visited Peru, with SG in 2014. This exactly when he came out at the International Airport in Peru and a group of fans were waiting for him and the band.

Justine Kores

Chris, thank you. We have been bonded from the beginning... I will miss your sweet voice and energy. I feel like my brother died... he did. Thank you for last summer. I'd never been in that dark a place... You were my beacon. I love you! Rest your worried mind... Rest your worried soul. You take a piece of me with you... Goodbye my Brother.

Karen Verbeek

Dear Chris, I am writing this one month after you found your place in Heaven. It hasn't become any easier to believe that you aren't here anymore. It will always be this way.

When I first heard your music, it was the background to a happy and exciting time in my life, as I was starting to live on my own (early 1990's). Your birthday is only one day after mine and it seemed like you were narrating elements of my own life. Later, your songs helped me understand what was happening within myself, and my family, as I went through a very difficult divorce and troubles with my children. They gave words to my feelings and your lyrics had more weight than other songs I was hearing.

About four years ago, I had a random thought to check if you had any solo albums. I went into the store and found *Songbook*. I have no idea why I did this? I hadn't been keeping up with what you were doing at all and I just thought, I miss that voice, I need to hear it! Later, I managed to get some of the last few tickets for the Songbook concert at Massey Hall. I was completely taken away to such a wonderful, sweet place with your music that night. The next year, I took my kids to Soundgarden. In 2015, I saw you again for your Higher Truth tour in Toronto. Another fantastic night when you gave your all. Do you remember the couple slow dancing in the aisle? There was so much love in that place that night.

I have the music to listen to, and photos to relive moments. How deeply I will miss seeing you here with us, doing what you loved so much. How very gifted, determined and committed you were and you have enriched us all. What helps to accept your passing is to see how many people share these feelings, and the art you have inspired in others. What you created and gave will always be loved and reveal new meanings in different times and situations. I am so happy that I rediscovered you in a new way later in life. Your dedication, extraordinary voice, incredible melodies and songs will always speak to me and touch my soul. I will sing them loudly with much love always.

Karen Whiteley Verbeek, Aurora, Canada.

Karey Hanson-Brennan

Letter to Chris Cornell   May 23, 2017

Somewhere in my dreams…

I can't get your words out of my head. Your music, over the years, has moved me and comforted me to the point where I feel like the wind has been knocked out of me. It's hard to breathe when I think of the loss of what's yet to come.

I've been a Soundgarden fan since 1989. By 1990, I would say I was a "superfan", couldn't get enough and saw the band every chance I got. I was devastated when the band broke up but I followed every project you were a part of. I saw Audioslave live, great music that came out of that time in your career. Your solo albums, the heartfelt lyrics you wrote, were like an insight into my soul. You basically have been there for me and impacted my life even though you didn't know it. As your music evolved, so did my life but I always connected with your lyrics. You seemed to understand my mind, so to speak. I think that's why this loss is so profound.

I met you once on your Euphoria Mourning tour in Detroit. I stood in a very long line, somewhat nervous, and finally shook your hand. I was so star struck, all I could say was… "You write great lyrics". Been kicking myself about that for years but I always thought I would get another chance to tell you… "Thank you. Your words and music have enriched my life and gotten me through some rough times. It has brought me great happiness, memories with friends and a scar from a mosh-pit. What I love about your lyrics most is that they are real. Thought provokingly, gut wrenching real. There is such beauty in your songs. Even the heartbreak, there is beauty in that too. Because you shared it with the world. Because you got through it. It's inspiring. It made ME stronger. You will always be an inspiration to me and the music will keep me going." Cheesy, I know, but true nonetheless.

I refuse to let the media change how I feel about all of this. Your passion for the music, your philanthropy, what I do know about you, the man, makes me believe it would have been quite something to know you. Soon, I will be able to talk about you without tearing up. I will tell people you are a poet, an advocate for change, a brilliant musician that will be forever remembered. You shared it with the world my friend. I hope that soon my sadness will fade a little and I will once again succumb to that haunting voice, those tones. Traces of your soul will forever live on that way. That gift you've given me, music that became a part of my identity. So, I hope, sorrow gives way to sunrise and life goes on to create new fans and share the music. Although I still can't wrap my head around the fact that you're gone from us, your memory, your music, will always remain in me.

R.I.P.

You will forever be the shape of the hole inside my heart.

KB

BY THE FANS AND FRIENDS OF CHRIS CORNELL

Photo: Karey Hanson-Brennan. Detroit, the final show.

Kari Reyes

I've been a fan of Soundgarden for so many years!! I first heard Chris's voice with Temple Of The Dog, and I was floored!! His voice was so powerful and moving. When I first heard *Badmotorfinger*, I couldn't believe my ears!! Chris's voice and lyrics resonated with me, and then seeing their videos on MTV was a sight to behold. And grunge had taken over my stereo!! I love how Eddie Vedder and Chris sound together. Even though I never had the chance to see Soundgarden live, I was still blessed beyond reason, always knowing that I can hear them any time I wanted.

Chris Cornell has made an impact on so many people, not only with his music but as a philanthropist too, with his contributions to help kids less fortunate. Chris Cornell will be greatly and sadly missed... no one can ever take his place.

Kasey Maynor

I've tried to find words to explain why the loss of someone I've never met makes me sad...

While I did not know Chris Cornell personally, my soul did. His voice held the key to my very existence, or so it felt. When he opened his mouth, nothing short of magic entered the atmosphere and permeated every ounce of my being. His music had a way of attaching itself as if by invisible strings to every emotion I never knew I was capable of feeling. It would flow through me and pull every string until there was nothing left to take. It was/is a once in a lifetime type of connection to another person's art that I fully believe will never happen again.

I was lucky enough to get to experience that magic live four times; twice as a solo act, and twice with Soundgarden. The first time as a solo act, I cried. Tears poured down my face as he sang "Say Hello to Heaven". The first time as Soundgarden, there were tornado warnings that day and we were at an outside venue. As the clouds rolled in and wind whipped everyone's hair, Cornell played the beginning notes to "Black Hole Sun". It was the single most amazing concert moment I have ever experienced. The second time solo was at The Ryman, the mother church, and it very much felt like a religious experience. It was the most connected I've ever felt to an artist's work. The second as Soundgarden, and last time I would ever get to experience the magic live, was just two weeks ago at a music festival. I had managed to be front row. As a huge fan of his, I am incredibly thankful that I got to experience those four moments. They were probably insignificant moments to him, just another show, but they have proven to be some of my favorite memories that I posses.

As a fan, the news of his death shocked and saddened me. And then came the news of it being self-inflicted. Suicide. Now not only am I shocked and saddened, but angry. Angry that we didn't have to lose him, that he took himself from us. From his family. From his friends. From the world. I can't help but think of his wife and his children, his family, to whom he seemed so devoted. And if I am saddened and shocked and angry, I cannot even begin to fathom what they must be feeling. My heart goes out to them.

And finally, SUICIDE IS NEVER THE ANSWER!!! Please, please, please, tell someone. Seek help. Hold on to hope. Because there is hope. There is always a sliver of light in the darkness, even if it is dim. There is always hope. YOU ARE IMPORTANT. YOU ARE LOVED.

I hope you are at peace Chris.

Kate Glencross

I saw Soundgarden for the first time in 2011 at the age of 21, after being a SG fan for years. It was at an outdoor venue where we tailgated beforehand, met new and old friends, and were ready for more after the show. The energy was awesome! "Burden In My Hand" got everyone pumped. I can still see the crowd when it started. It was one of my top five concerts I've ever been to, and will remain in that range.

Saw SG again in 2013 indoors, had a different but great experience. Funny how being indoors can change a heavy band's performance without dulling their sound. Finally saw him solo in 2015 during his Higher Truth tour, with that show being in my top five as well. I didn't buy *Higher Truth* on CD until last summer, but it's been in my CD player non-stop ever since.

For someone who loves sad songs, he knocked it out of the park again with this album, and spoke to me, and millions of others, in a dark and beautiful way. Between his words in interviews, lyrics, unique style and his art in general, Chris is a huge loss that won't be replaced in my lifetime, and I'm thankful for the memories of seeing him. I can only hope my children have an artist like him in their lifetime, but they will grow up with his music, as his legacy will live on.

Thank You ~ Kate

Photo: Pixabay

Kathy Nieboer

I know that I am not the only one who feels a horrible darkness since you chose to leave this world.

I fell in love with your music in the beginning days of Soundgarden. I was a huge fan of Black Sabbath when I found my own rock and roll path. I would listen to an 8 track of *Paranoid*. I would sit for hours and hours to hear "Fairies Wear Boots", then Led Zeppelin, The Rolling Stones, all of the greatest bands. My mother had a great collection of albums, and I could get lost in the music... playing each record until I knew every word. I think that is where my love of those dark guitars came from.

When Soundgarden came along years later the music resonated the same way... Your words seemed to put me in a trance... I could sway, or lay on the floor in a dark place and escape from the reality that was mine.

Great bands did not visit Hawaii very much... but Soundgarden came in 1997, I think. My best friend and I dressed in our/her best leather corsets, jeans, and boots to get downtown Honolulu to see the band play. The arena was full. I was lost in your gorgeousness. Your voice just vibrated my soul. The show ended abruptly... people started to leave. I was outraged that the lights came on!!! I was screaming for people to sit down, they are not done... they are not done, I screamed over and over. Sit the fuck down!!! There may even have been some spitting. I was furious!!! It wasn't until years later that I found out that it was equipment failure and lots of frustration between members of the band. My best friend and I could have gotten ourselves hurt, badly for acting so crazy, but... I did not care. I cared about hearing you and the boys singing my favorite songs.

I lived in a dark life full of abuse and addictions for many years. Your song "Four Walled World" allowed to me to believe there may be light at the end of the tunnel. "She'll be gone when the sun hits the ground"... You call me a dog... "Black Hole Sun" was a theme song for me while trying to escape one of those relationships... "Mailman"... how many times did I play that song hoping that he would one day he may feel as horribly as he made me feel?

I could go one and on sharing with you the silent empowerment your words and melodies gave me. Light to my darkness, love to my hate. When I did not want to take one more breath, I would have rather been in fire than breathe... your music shared hope, love, and light. I escaped all the pain, sadness, and darkness of life. Your music carried me along the way.

I have travelled with others, or alone to see Soundgarden. I have travelled to see you alone. You, your guitars, and a red phone. I fell in love with the record player again listening to your opening... the crackle of the vinyl... watching you play. Adoring your stories of what, and the why of the songs. I fell in love with the way that you tilt your head when you belt out those powerful words. I was afraid to blink fearing I would miss your smile. I have met wonderful people because of our love of your music. Your music has encompassed my life, it will always encompass my life. I have never cried as I have cried since you passed. I still mourn. I do not judge you for how you chose to leave this earth. I hope that you now know what you meant to so many. I hope that you can see that we sing your songs loud. I hope you don't mind that some of us cannot hit the notes, yet sing them anyway. I will never stop. I heard that you wanted to make a record with an orchestra... that would have been amazing. I will miss getting the emails that you are coming to a town near me with others, or alone. I will miss the long drives with the radio up and the windows down to hear you play.

Please know that you were a gift to this world, a gift to me. I will make sure to carry your legacy of music until the day I leave this earth, thank you for leaving so much music. Just one more thing... what made you the most sexy, is that you could have had any woman in this world, they would have lined up for you, yet you only shared your life with Vicky. I could see your love for her in pictures. As a woman, that is how we hope our men would look at us, only us.

Thank you, Chris Cornell.

Katy Banteah

This has been a rough past few days. I can't find the right words to describe this big feeling of loss. Feels like a family member died. Today was the first day I could listen to him without crying. I even broke down at work the day after it happened when I heard "Thank You" playing.
    All of you... Thanks for sharing, mourning, all your thoughts are a big help in trying to heal or deal? I guess. We're all going through this. He was the voice, our hero, Rock God, for the ladies our dream guy with the gorgeous looks and a golden voice to match. And so much more, of course. So much more... You all know.
    This Friday will be tough for us. He left his heart and music for us. Just continue to rock out and absorb the lyrics, music and voice he left us with always. I could go on and on but... Rest in peace CC. I never wanted to write these words down for you.... and thanks, you all are the best. He had/has the best fans ever...

Kellen Morse

I felt I needed to say something. I listened to Chris when growing up so much that it's not just like he's some singer who passed away. He was from my hometown. He went to the high school my best friend goes to, granted many years prior. Chris is not just a musician, he's a humanitarian and will forever remain a legend. Rest easy brother, we'll miss you.

THANK YOU: A TRIBUTE TO CHRIS CORNELL

Artwork: Csaba Mester

Kelly McFadyen

I grew up in West Auckland, New Zealand. During the late 80's & 90's 'grunge' styles and music was rampant. I'd heard and seen Soundgarden on TV, always intrigued with that topless guy with all the hair... However it wasn't until eight years ago that Chris began to make a real impact. I really started listening...

I was in a toxic relationship that eventually changed me in an awful way. Every time I didn't think I could last another day, I would hear "Be Yourself" on the radio. This started to become a recurring thing. "Be Yourself" found me everywhere. Finally my toxic ex moved out. I was broke, but I had a happy, peaceful home - and a LOT of Audioslave. I got *Be Yourself* tattooed on my foot, as it was Chris who helped me find my feet again. Then I had a LOT of Soundgarden!

Chris' music envelops me in a blanket of safety. And gives me a boost or kick up the ass when needed.

My eldest daughter surprised me with a trip to Australia so as I could finally see my hero. And it was the best time of my life. I was lucky enough to see him here in Auckland twice for the Higher Truth tour, and lucky enough to win an autographed image of him. Just looking at it now, knowing that his hands have touched an item I own, fills me with peace.

THANK YOU: A TRIBUTE TO CHRIS CORNELL

At age 43, I decided to go to university to get a degree in Social Anthropology - I'm now in my second year. I owe a huge thank you to Chris and Vicky and their love of people, for me wanting to be a better person and to support those who need it most. Millions of hearts have broken this week, but Chris you will be with us forever.

Xx Much love from NZ.

Kera Berutti

Only an Angel

Only an angel could have a voice like yours
Melt your heart
Send shivers
Give goosebumps
Bring you back to your happy place
Or your rock bottom
Touch the hearts of millions without ever physically being together
Together...
That's what an angel makes you feel
Only an angel could make you feel connected to them from afar
Only an angel would share this gift
The gift of song, of love, of hate, of regret
Your gift of familiarity, knowing within the first note it was your angelic voice
Only an angel could share this gift
Right up till the very end

THANK YOU: A TRIBUTE TO CHRIS CORNELL

The end...
Your last performance...
I was with you, in that same room
Screaming your name, singing along, throwing up peace signs and hearts, sending my love
Only an angel wouldn't need that love
Angels aren't here to receive love, but to radiate it
Make us feel part of something grand, bigger than ourselves
Only an angel would make me feel strong and delicate. Empowered and fragile.
Only an angel can lift you up
If only this angel could have stayed longer

-Kera Berutti

Kerrie Dixon

A light in the universe went out the day Chris left this world, but the angels are rejoicing as our loss is surely their gain and wherever they all are they can listen to his voice for all eternity. We will do our best to relight the brightly burning flame that was Chris Cornell ~ husband, father, brother, son, friend, saviour of so many lost and troubled souls. Good night Chris, sleep well.

Kerrie and Aiden xxxxx

THANK YOU: A TRIBUTE TO CHRIS CORNELL

Photo: Piera Alessio

Kimberly Bennett

This is something I wrote on Chris' page after a show in 2013. We were in front row and it was so amazing. Life-altering, as he has always been in my life.

I've been a fan since the late 80's and have absolutely loved everything you have done. There is a song with your voice on it for every stage of my life. I have seen you seven times but last night was the most special, maybe because I have never been so close to you, first row but also because of the surprise for my youngest daughter. All my children (and now grandchildren) grew up with your music and now my youngest daughter plays your songs on her guitar. She is turning 17 next week so I gave her this gift as an early birthday present. And as a complete surprise. She cried when she read the marquee as we arrived to Balboa Theatre and she kept asking, "Is this real?"

You moved us with your passion, your intensity and limitless, unparalleled talent. I continue to be stunned by you. We spent almost three hours within feet of you and I could see every nuance in your face, mouth, eyes, hands and body, the way you shift leg positions at certain points of songs, it's all so "right now". I thought, wow, that man is truly in the

MOMENT. Your passion for what you were doing was evident through every fiber of your being. I looked at one point and realized to myself that you are like a child right now, right here. As you busied yourself at the end, setting up things, effects on the pedalboard and the guitar, I watched intently and saw this little boy with so much concentration put into the immediate task. Like a kid setting up a train set and it has to be PERFECT! You know? I mean, wow, I want that. I want to see that in myself. And through all the passion and intensity, light and humor, and so many smiles and laughs as you run your hands through that tangle of hair, I was overwhelmed at how much you LOVE what you do!! You love it.

This is what makes you so special to me. The passion is pure and the focus and emotion is like nothing I've ever seen. At least not consistently. Show after show after year after decades. You truly love what you do and that makes all the difference. There is no way to properly thank you for all you've given me and my family. My daughter even got to hold your guitar after the show and got a hand squeeze from you, too. I came in too late. Maybe next time! For now, I need to get back to my art, my writing, and my music. Thank you for reminding me that I need to make time to do what I love.

Kimmie Andersen

Thank you, Chris, for being you, and having the ability to express yourself in such a direct, in-your-face way, but also with such feeling and beautiful fragility. Not many artists can do that, and reach such a broad audience as you did.

I have listened to your music since I was 10-12 years old. I just turned 40 a couple of days before you passed. So you have pretty much been in my life forever, along with Temple Of The Dog, Soundgarden, Audioslave, Chris Cornell solo and the surrounding groups.

I have the same diagnosis as you did, so I understood your pain and sensitivity to life, the world and other people. It's a blessing and a curse, because it gives you a great insight to other people, and yourself. But it also leaves you extremely vulnerable to everything around you.

I'm heartbroken that you are gone, especially the way you chose to go. But I also know that you are free now, and feel no pain inside.

I actually don't think you knew just how loved you really were (are) by everyone, fans, family, friends and fellow musicians. But you are, and always will be! You left a big hole in the world, and no one can fill it out after you, that black hole is yours for ever.

I will think of you and do something to remember you twice every year now, on May 18, where you sadly left us. And on July 20, when you were born into this world and helped make it beautiful with your amazing voice and your incredible musical talent. Not to forget your pure and gentle personality, that shone through everything you did.

I know your biggest worry is your three kids, and I'm sure they will be very well looked after. And they will be able to smile again, when the dark clouds are gone. But it will probably be a little while yet.

Again, thank you for everything you have given all of us, for all these years. It will be a part of us forever.

Rest in peace Chris!

Love from Kimmie Andersen, Copenhagen, Denmark.

Kris Andrade

I was fortunate enough to get to see his Songbook concert tour here in Saskatoon, Canada many years ago.

During the show he was passing these out as the show progressed and many people were starting to fight to get them. Slipping on wet floors and getting hurt wasn't really what I had come there for so I just resigned myself to the fact I wasn't going to be able to get one. Chris had dedicated a song to his wife that night and as the mosh pit had calmed down to the point of being able to slowly wind my way closer to the front of the stage, I found myself almost right beside him.

When Chris was finished, he lifted his head and saw me... he looked at me standing there (probably a little star struck to be honest) and he never said anything as he grabbed my hand and pressed this pick into the palm of my right hand and then closed it with both of his. I held my prize up to show my wife, as well as everyone else who saw him give it to me. My smile was bigger than I could have ever thought possible to achieve, but just before he grabbed another pick we locked eyes for a second and I mouthed a fast "thank you" he said "you're welcome" and brought the house down with "You Know My Name"... one could never forget his name.

Krista Strogilis Bramon

It was so crazy, but I made it. For months my friends who know me and my following of CC kept harassing me that I was going to miss his show and I had to keep replying that I cannot because it is Mother's Day and I'm gonna be with my children. The Thursday before the show (four days before) I was in New Jersey visiting my sister when one more friend called freaking out that I'm not going to go and I cannot miss him. At that moment I thought *you know what, I will ask my 10-year-old son what he would think about going to his very first concert and seeing Mommy's number one favorite in the whole world* and he actually was excited. $233 later all I could think of was how insane I was but if we were going to have a special Mother's Day, sons first, CC kind of time - we were doing it right. I tear up just at how thankful I am for that $233 spent. Knowing, I would have cleared accounts and more. Life is short.

I was at the KC concert, second to last. My son and I stood at the stage, Chris came over twice to give my son some of his picks and shook his hand. My son was elated and I was beyond, whatever that word may be, lol.

BY THE FANS AND FRIENDS OF CHRIS CORNELL

Photos: Krista Strogilis Bramon

Kristin Sanna Imperiale

I can't wrap my mind around this. My heart is so broken and so few around me truly get the pain. Didn't he know how much we loved him? Not for his looks, but his genius. He was a gift every time he stepped on the stage. He sounded better and more consistent vocally in later years. I'm devastated. Truly broken hearted.

L.S.

Chris: Just wanted you to know... The girl that got away and I were once talking and then one of your songs started playing. We looked at each other and smiled. She told me a joke and in that moment I fell for her. In the time we were together we always listened to that song and talked about that moment. Now every time I listen to you, I remember her. And I think that is beautiful. Thank you for that.

L.S., 34, Chile.

Laurie Rosso

Dear Chris,

It's incredibly difficult to accept that your journey in this lifetime is over. You've been the main constant in my life since I first heard you sing so many years ago. Since then your music has literally been the soundtrack of my life. I have been blessed many times over when it comes to you and I cherish all of it... every minute, every second, in your presence. Going on without you seems impossible, but somehow it will happen. You may be gone, but you will NEVER be forgotten. Your music will always be with me... in my heart and soul. It's in my veins and will always be contagious.

Leo Petrovski

What have you done, my giant spark?

Seeing "Jesus Christ Pose" video for the first time changed my taste in music forever. It was something fresh and really new and hit right in the needed spot of my music sensitivity. It wasn't heavy metal anymore but the progress. I fell in love with Soundgarden that much so I joined The Knights of the Sound Table fan club, despite living in Russia, which troubled the mail correspondence with the outside world in those pre-internet times.

Then Chris cut his hair and wrote that best-of-all-times song "Black Hole Sun". The album has been just an explosion for me and is still modern sounding nowadays, bearing the title of direction in which Chris has gone in May of 2017 – The *Superunknown*. *Euphoria Morning* and *Carry On* made me survive two lethal diseases so I am still alive and he isn't. That's an impact. The loss I will probably never recover from.

"Wide Awake" recently got me in tears where Chris is screaming "Wide Awake!" several times in the end of the song at the top of his power. We all should have been wide awake to not let him go. And we are all guilty of the crime of sleeping at this time.

Thank you my dear Chris. I built a yacht and named it

"Sunshower". If you see it from above one day, know it's your song sailing. I will miss you forever.

Photo: Dawn Belotti

Leslie Cross

Thank you Chris for all the wonderful music you created. Music has always been so important to me. Music means so many things, life, love, sadness, joy and a way for us to express ourselves. I am so saddened by your loss, it makes me wish that somehow we could go back in time and try and help you. You meant the world to so many people and we thank you for sharing yourself with us. I thank you... someday we will all meet and there will be the best concert ever happening. I'll make sure I'm front and center.

Sincerely, Leslie.

Photo: Dawn Belotti

With Soundgarden, Hammerstein, January 23, 2013.

Lilly Dunne

Dear Chris,
    The world has lost an angel and is a little darker without you here. Your music saved me as a messed up kid, and I've been a devoted super fan ever since. I've been blessed to see you many times down here in Melbourne, once you even stopped to sing to me... a memory I will cherish for the rest of my life. You made us all feel like your friend, and as such, I mourn you in that respect.
    Rest In Peace beautiful man, the demons won't bother you anymore.
    With much love,
    Lilly Dunne, Melbourne, Australia.

THANK YOU: A TRIBUTE TO CHRIS CORNELL

Lily Rodriguez McLoughlin

It's surreal that he is gone. I have been a fan since 1993. Each time I see him now I still cannot believe it. I do take comfort though in the fact that what he left us, the fans, the lovers of all things Chris Cornell, is a vast and extensive treasure trove of music, many collaborations and interviews. There he will forever be alive. I saw an interview just last night, and to see him laugh and share made me very happy. It won't bring him back by any means but in the end we have it, along with the camaraderie of loving him.

Lisa Dalachinsky

I felt compelled to write something regarding the immense impact the death of Chris Cornell has had on me. It's been seven days since he took his life away and it's all I have been able to think about. I'm shocked at the fact that I can't seem to get it out of my head. Like a bad dream! It has consumed me, so much that it's somewhat abnormal. I have scoured the internet and social media sites to read everything I possibly can about him. "You don't know how important someone is to you as an artistic influence until suddenly they're gone. I've certainly been having that experience." - Chris Cornell.

I was lucky enough to see SOUNDGARDEN a couple of times but was not a crazy super-obsessed fan! I do love the music though!

It's strange how hearing a song can immediately take you back to a moment in time. His music, particularly his voice, had a profound impact on my life. It brought me up and down, allowed me to get lost in the words and sound. His "lion" roar was depressing, sexy, seductive, dark, hopeful, and uplifting all at the same time.

He spoke to me during a transitional time in my life when I moved from Pittsburgh to South Florida to "start over" not knowing a soul. Like Chris, for a period in my life I drank enough to forget. In 1994 my roommate and I spent countless hours listening to Soundgarden. We used to walk around the lake and I would say "One More Time Around" and she would say "Might Do It". Like Chris I got my shit together. I went to graduate school, became a teacher, and met "my soulmate" who "saved my life".

Fast forward 20+ years, his music still speaks to me. I still work in the same school but I now coordinate services for students with disabilities. Like Chris I have a daughter (13) who is about the same age as his middle child Toni. In this crazy political world where the government is cutting money from social issues, the arts, the economically disadvantaged, and mental health, I'm hoping that something good can come out of this tragic loss. I'm hopeful that Chris Cornell's unnecessary, untimely death will shed a powerful light on the need to address and fund social issues.

I feel so, so sad for his family and friends. I wish that "the butterfly effect" could have taken place and Chris wasn't left alone to his own demons! I think that his death has had such a profound impact on myself and his other fans because we all saw a little of ourselves in him. It hurts so bad and cuts so deep because it didn't have to happen and it seemed to all of us like he made it through, that he overcame his demons and if it happened to him it could happen to us! What a sad, sad, sad loss for all of us! "Say Hello To Heaven"!

Lisa Dalachinsky.

Lisa McCaffrey

There are many stars that shine but you shone like no other, and I know and you will shine again for generations to come. I felt your soul was as hauntingly beautiful as your lyrics. You blew me away with your stage presence, those eyes, that howling, powerful voice, it capitulated all before you and it is true "nobody sings like you anymore". Thank You!

Lisa Moore Corley

My Chris story... when I was 19, I met Chris Cornell - way back in 1990 - went to see Soundgarden, Faith No More and Voivod. Soundgarden was amazing. After their set, I bought a CD from Chris who was at the merch table. He and another guy went into the bar and were watching the show as me and my friends went into the pit. I got kicked in the face and went down hard. Who pulled me out of the pit - Chris Cornell. He and whoever was with him helped me to the bar, got me ice for my broken nose and sat with me for about 20 minutes. He was the kindest man.

After that I devotedly followed his career and went to every show I could when they visited Atlanta. I missed his last show here, which was on May 3rd, because I wanted to wait for new music. When I read the news of his passing at 6am at my desk at work I remember hoping that it was terrible mistake. When I realized it wasn't, I started to cry. I really felt a profound loss. I didn't know him other that through his music and my one brush with him and yet the profound sadness has lingered. I'm glad that my grief was similar to so many and I hope he is at peace. How lucky I was to have my experience and to cling to his amazing music. There will never be another quite as wonderful.

Lisa Ryan

Obviously his lyrics, music, voice, great looks and love for his family made Chris exceptional. But it was during his Songbook tour he was like a good friend. Chillin', playing guitar, telling stories. So humble and funny. One of us. So easy to love! That's my favorite memory.

Lisa Vickers

THANK YOU: A TRIBUTE TO CHRIS CORNELL

BY THE FANS AND FRIENDS OF CHRIS CORNELL

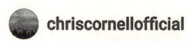 **chriscornellofficial**

Liked by **eddieismyway, tonivasil1** and 3,525 others

chriscornellofficial Lyric graphic from Lisa Vickers Aspen 2015 #fanartfriday

See also page 259.

Liz Eismendi

Thank You Chris Cornell. Your music was a blessing to my soul and will sing forever in my heart.

Lloyd Hendricks

Photo: Lloyd Hendricks

THANK YOU: A TRIBUTE TO CHRIS CORNELL

Photo: Lloyd Hendricks

Lois Giles

It was sometime in early 90's. I was married with a son and didn't get out much... lived in a small shithole town, with shithole people. I happened to win some sort of local radio station promo thing, so I strapped my little boy on my back and went down there.

Out of some car, I hear this most amazing, rock belting, zero fucks given voice and I was stopped dead in my tracks. As I wandered over to this car full of guys, which I'm sure they were thinking *what the hell is this mom with a kid on her back want?* with her mall bangs and preppy shirt on... but see I was just like them, only I was married, living a life that fucks were supposed to be given, to please other people... As I sat with these guys, and listened to you sing, wail mostly, I knew something in me had changed forever... As I left there, your voice echoed in my head like a starburst that had hit my soul... Yes, I was forever changed... The next day I was down at the local record store, after digging my Doc Martens back out of the closet, wearing my husband's flannel and not giving zero fucks...

You and I grew together, we battled together, we won together and we lost together, as we were the same age... You have been in my life for 27 years, and I thank you for showing me when to give zero fucks, and when to give to most fucks... Your music will forever be a part of my life, my children's life, who now have kids of their own, and your legacy will live forever. See, you gave me something to keep pushing on for, always, even when I didn't want to. I feel that way now, but I will continue, because I have every single thing you have ever published to keep me going, and I am humbled to be alive and in this universe and share your space, the same time with you,

Forever and always...
Before we Disappear...
Lois Giles

Lucas Santos

I've lost my best friend...
Though I never met him,
he knew just who I am.
Not in a physical way,
but as the words left his mouth
I could relate, and realise he knew me.
That was my best friend.
During my life, he saved some of my friends.
Friend of a friend.
A lapse of conscience would throw me off this raft,
but his voice and words are there to fill the gap.
Take over, get lost, then take over again.
My friend showed me the way.
"How to Live" was my favorite chapter of the book,
the one he wrote, called "Go and Save Yourself".
It's been pretty empty since he fell.
It is easier to drown since I'm alone on this raft.
There's no balance. Drown me in you.
I got lost time and time again, but I never take over.

That is life without my best friend...
And...
I've lost my best friend.

Photo: Pixabay

Lucy Clifton Sims

Woke up to "Be Yourself" in my head this morning... Thank you, Chris, for everything you gave us. You live eternally in our hearts. Goodbye beautiful soul.

THANK YOU: A TRIBUTE TO CHRIS CORNELL

Lucy Hannaford

A lion roared at me in 1994 one day,
He screamed to my soul that he'd had a black day,
The curls, the passion, the fire within you,
Ripped through my heart, my brain, every sinew,
Who was this man? This God full of talent and on a spiritual mission,
I fell hard and loved you, that is my only admission,
I was intrigued, I needed to know who you were,
Why were you inside me, the obsession I could not deter,
A teenage mind, so confused, found a light, an angel to follow,
My heart has been full ever since and I'm scared to feel hollow.
Please don't leave, tell me you're going to stay
We promised, we would, always follow your way,
How or why we may never answer but I don't want to get over you,
I'm awash reliving my life full of you, but God the pain,
You saved me from myself as I danced in your Steel Rain,
Your highs and your lows we have been there no matter, but it seems you are done,
Arms held out, you were the only one,
The ugly truth is sinking in – maybe we really have lost you,

THANK YOU: A TRIBUTE TO CHRIS CORNELL

Alive into the Superunknown you flew,
But remember sweet man of the world who grieves for you,
A room a thousand years wide with a rain splattered view,
You didn't want to go, you were not in your right mind,
Remember, my love, you will never be outshined.

Lyn Shelle

Thank You for your amazing way of connecting with others through your music. Your voice has touched many souls. And marked our hearts forever. I thought I had something special with your music and concerts connecting me with my sister. A special bond. But since your passing I see the bond you have had with so many, in so many ways. They say your music and your openness saved them. Now I can only hope that all of us coming together and sharing our story... will connect us and bond us to not let your death go without a higher meaning.

Rest In Peace Dearest Chris. Thank you for the Amazing Memories. We will not let you down. We "Promise".

Maggie Partridge

My memories of you consist of crazy, intoxicating, euphoric live shows, and I was never drunk or high because I didn't want to miss a thing. I remember the rumblings back in 1989 of how amazing your live shows were. I had to see this for myself. In a small venue in Vancouver, BC, back in March 4, 1992 at the Commodore, you blew my mind. I was completely hooked. Your presence was raw, angry, dark, yet sexually energizing and addictive.

I saw you again at Lollapalooza July 21, 1992 at Thunder Bird Stadium in Vancouver. It was a mud fest that day, Doc Martens, long wet hair and flannel everywhere. It always rains in the northwest but we were diehards a little rain never stopped us.

I saw you again seven times. The last concert at the Orpheum on September 30, 2015. I wish I knew that would be the last time. I would have made sure to not take for granted you would always be here.

I will always hold love and respect for you as an artist, musician, a father and a great human being. The day you died, a piece of our hearts died. There will never be another like you, ever!

Rest in peace Dark Knight.

Mari Brown

Thank you Chris for the music you wrote, dark feelings you share… all got me through troubled times. Where most made me feel crazy, you made me feel normal. Loyalty is infinity! Rest In Paradise Chris Cornell. You are the sky.

You did reach down, and lifted the crowd up.

Maricruz Rowley

My story in short: I remember being around seven years old and listening to "Black Hole Sun" on the radio. I remember being very intrigued. At 14, I discovered who Chris was and the love affair began. I could listen to him read the phonebook.

Cut to 2013. I've never been wealthy, I've always had to work hard for everything. So when I heard Soundgarden would be in NC I went into a panic, because I knew since I supported myself at the time on a minimum wage job there would be no way I could afford tickets. Then, as if fate existed, my work started this weight loss competition. Long story short, I lost 30 pounds in three months and won the money for the trip. Starved myself, exercise.

Get to the day of the concert, two hours before they were supposed to go on the venue cancelled because of rain. This past month they were here again. This time I didn't get to go because me and my husband just had a baby, and everybody knows how hard it is to do anything when you're responsible for a little one.

Hindsights 20/20 had I known, I'd have made time, found money. I can't begin to describe what I feel right now. I have his words tattooed on my back. Regardless of what happened, Chris will forever be a part of my life. Thanks for everyone's

support, fuck money.
    Sad in NC.

Photo: Dawn Belotti

Marisa Cassiano

It has been a month since you're gone but it seems like yesterday. I couldn't imagine it would hurt me so much.

I thought I was the last bittersweet type of person on the planet. What a pretence of mine! Then I discovered you, who knew to merge heavy with delicate like no one else.

It was horrible to wake up with that bunch of messages that day. It was horrible to open all of them and realize what had happened. It was horrible trying to find out if it was truth. It was horrible to read the answer... It was horrible to feel... It was horrible to know how everything happened and imagine it.

You were invincible to me. Actually, you still are because "no one sings like you anymore". The world will miss you.

Marisa Cassiano – Brazil.

Maureen Wells

I have followed CC from the beginning. My son Josh was born in 1980 and he and I had a mutual love of anything CC . We went to concerts together, listened to his music together. CC got both of us through the good and the bad. Josh passed away in 2005 and I needed all things CC... I listened non-stop for what turned into months, and without CC am not quite sure I would have made it through to the other side. And be able to deal with my life without Josh. From that point on if I was sad or upset thinking about Josh I could always call on CC to help me through and make me feel close to Josh. I felt that was my one connection that remained with my son.

Now that CC has gained his wings and is flying free I feel lost once again, like that connection has been broken and am quite lost. At some point I will reconcile to my new reality but will always miss the one connection I felt I still had with my son.

The world has lost a beautiful human being, a wonderful musician, writer and person. Godspeed Chris Cornell. May your soul find the peace your were always searching for.

Meg Kenning

I learned as soon as I woke up yesterday but didn't let myself really feel it until I dropped the kids off at school. I went right down to a bench where I like to sit overlooking the beach. I go there when I'm sad, stressed, happy, or just need to just be. I cried and watched a video of "Man of Golden Words" at TOTD Philly night two —the last time I saw him perform. He introduces it talking about Andy and how shattered he was at his death and they tagged "Comfortably Numb". I never saw Andy live and Chris was my Man of Golden Words.

I went to a bench overlooking the water and tried to process it but couldn't. When I got home I added "The Keeper" lyrics to a photo I took and made it my cover photo. I interpret "The Keeper" to mean I will keep his memory alive. I will play his music for my children and continue to spin it all the time. I plan to keep it as my cover photo for weeks. Right now I have a photo up honoring that tomorrow is the anniversary of when we brought my daughter home from the adoption agency but I will switch back to this one after.

Updated my cover photo last night to black after all the Chris sites did. While very sad, I thought it was a beautiful, united tribute. It's hard to believe it's been a week. I posted "Zero Chance" lyrics with my black cover. Listening to it this morning and this song is incredibly sad right now especially the chorus. Yet it remains a favorite of mine and, oddly, comforts me.

Melina Pereira Vai

Here's a happy story.

I've been a hardcore Soundgarden fan for a while (I used to be Soundgarden_girl on the Soundgarden world forums, if you used to go on there, hi!). Anyway, in 2011 I heard Chris Cornell was going to be performing his new song "The Keeper" on the Letterman Show and I knew I had to try to get tickets to see him perform. Anyway, to win the tickets you had to call the morning of and answer a trivia question about the show, since I never really watched Letterman religiously I studied questions about the show all night long. I ended up calling, answering the question correctly and getting two free Letterman tickets for me and my husband. We were so ecstatic to see Chris live!

So on the day of the show, I had to take a train to New York City and as usual the Long Island railroad was running behind. The ride, which usually takes 45 minutes, ended up taking an hour and I got there too late. They said they could no longer let us in. I was devastated. I told my husband I didn't want to give up yet and we decided to just wait outside the door, because who knows maybe we'd see Chris from a distance and, lo and behold, about an hour later we saw him.

He was about to get in his car and I started screaming at the top of my lungs "CHRIS, CHRIS!" and he came over. He was so nice, I asked for a picture he said yes.

My husband and I came to the conclusion that if we had actually got there on time and gone inside to the taping of the Letterman Show, there's no way we would've been able to meet Chris outside. So everything happens for a reason... sometimes you're sad over something that happened in your life but you never know it might just be paving the way towards something even better.

Thank you Chris!! This was seriously one of the best days of my life, I love the picture, he looks genuinely happy.

THANK YOU: A TRIBUTE TO CHRIS CORNELL

Melissa Christensen

I love the fact that my words are coming back. I use to write poetry but it has been many years since I could get it out of my head and down on paper. Thank you Chris for inspiring me again.

THANK YOU: A TRIBUTE TO CHRIS CORNELL

His music was our medication, our cure for that moment. When we felt lost and confused. A simple note sang to lift us up or the lion roar to let us express the pain. He left us with so many emotions connected through his songs. How did he know the right thing to sing?

I am grateful for the music, the angelic voice he had, the powerful meanings. His vessel on this earth may be gone but his spirit will continue to live through all of us.

I wish you could've stayed a bit longer.
I wish you could've known the impact you had.
I wish you blessings in the sky.
I wish you peace.

Much love our angel Chris.

Melissa Christensen

BY THE FANS AND FRIENDS OF CHRIS CORNELL

Since you left I have become so numb
This life has turned cumbersome.
Devastated by such heartache
With pain that I can not shake

No tears roll down my face
As my eyes are too dry to embrace

You came into our lives strong and free
The way the lord made you to be
To touch our souls and minds
With words in song that we couldn't find

No tears roll down my face
As my eyes are too dry to embrace

When time comes for us to understand
We will be suffering in a wasteland
For when the tears fall from my eyes
Floods will pour as I begin to cry

As only my heart remembers your face
You have become a memory in its place

By: Melissa Christensen
05/21/2017

Melissa Mazzoni Clark

Last Thursday morning as I was holding back the tears, I had to tell my seven year old that Chris Cornell died. Her response was so sweet, "I'm sorry momma, now you don't have a boyfriend anymore" (keep in mind I am married to her father, so we would joke that CC was my boyfriend). Then she said, "I guess you'll never be able to take me to see him in concert like you promised..." It is amazing how many people he touched that a seven year old could love his music too. "Murderer of Blue Skies" is her favorite song...

Mia B. Becker

I was born in 1988, so unfortunately, a few years too young during the explosion of the "Seattle" sound. However, I discovered Nirvana at the age of 10, which lead to my discovery of Soundgarden and Chris Cornell. He is my favorite of all time and one of my greatest loves for as long as I can remember. His eyes, his voice, well... everything, for almost 20 years. A one of a kind voice, dark brilliance and complexity of his lyrics, song writing abilities, arrangement, and again his voice.

Fast forward, I started high school when Audioslave released their self-titled album in November 2002, and graduated once Audioslave disbanded. Audioslave's first album is (still) one of my favorites, and is a very special time for me. It created an opportunity for me to finally see Chris Cornell live in concert.

My first Chris Cornell show was in March 2003, in New York. I remember everything about that show, but watching Chris Cornell hit that note in "Cochise" will forever be burned into my memory. Following that first show, I was lucky to have seen Chris live many times after that between 2003-2016 - 21 times in total across Chris' career: Audioslave, solo, Soundgarden, and Temple of The Dog. Every show was special in its own way.

On May 18, 2017, just after 1am in Los Angeles, I heard the news of Chris' very sudden and tragic passing. My heart physically hurts from the loss. I am heartbroken and devastated. However, I am thankful to have so much of Chris' music that embodies his talent, and beautiful spirit that will live on forever, and my memories of his 21 shows will last me a lifetime.

Chris, No one sings like you anymore.

Mia B. Becker, 29, Los Angeles, CA.

Michael J. Falotico

Being 52 and a poet/artist my inspiration has always been drawn from music. The death of John Lennon was a huge loss for me and leaves a hole in my heart of all we could of seen in his later years. Losing Chris this week has had that equal affect on me. Being the same age as Chris I so much related to his lyrics and now another hole in my heart has been made.

I hope he has finally found his peace. Thank you Chris for the inspiration and the life that helped moved my pen as well.

Poet Mike

Inside The Scream

A voice silenced but still heard...
The impact of cries spill from my words...
A life battled, a life inspired through song...
The fight inside is seldom spoken just left alone...
From the range in his vocals to the passive fear in his eyes...
Understood and felt through the heartfelt goodbyes...
The tears fall for memories of when, a poet inspired because you moved his pen...

THANK YOU: A TRIBUTE TO CHRIS CORNELL

Photo: Dawn Belotti – with Soundgarden, Hammerstein, January 23, 2013.

Michelle Deffinger

Maybe once in a lifetime
someone will make a difference
Touch your soul so personally
reach into your heart

You may not even realize
how big a part they play
You just enjoy their presence
feeling comforted by their voice

Music is powerful in many ways
as a means to escape and soothe
Providing support and strength
becoming our personal coach

Chris is both that someone
who made a difference
as well as that powerful musician
coaching others through life

THANK YOU: A TRIBUTE TO CHRIS CORNELL

I say 'is' because he still lives
in our hearts and souls
He left so many gifts to cherish
for years to come

His beautiful spirit lives on
in his music and other work
He made a difference to many
and we leaned on him like a crutch

Someone once said
maybe we leaned to hard
It got to be too much for him
holding us all up

It couldn't have been easy
but he was true and honest
We could feel that coming from him
and that's why we love him so

No words and no tribute
could ever be enough
To thank this man
who was a gift to so many

But maybe together
as fans and friends
We can attempt to return
a giant comforting thank you to share for years to come

Michelle Evans & Diana Walker

Since the beginning... Forever in our hearts.

With love, Michelle Evans & Diana Walker.

Michelle Sharp

The morning of May 18, 2017, I woke the same as any other day except a Facebook message from my friend John showed up on my phone, it said, "OMG... Cornell". My heart stopped then started pounding uncontrollably and I could not catch my breath as I knew what that message surely meant. I looked on Facebook and read the unimaginable. The gut-wrenching feeling of pain for Chris after reading how, nearly made me collapse.

Nearly one month later and I do not feel any less shocked or heartbroken. One day has not passed by that I have not shed a tear. I feel like I'm living in an alternate universe. Chris leaving us suddenly, like that, now, just seems unreal. I will forever keep his kids, family and friends in my thoughts and prayers. My heart and soul ache for his kids.

I had the pleasure of meeting Chris in 2007 at a 'Meet and Greet' in Minneapolis on a beautiful summer night on the roof of a restaurant. He seemed uncomfortable with the whole process as he sat in the middle of his band. I could feel his unease but he was gracious and I felt his gentle nature. I started talking to him but went mute when I looked in to his beautiful green eyes, always thought they were blue. I was overwhelmed and had no idea what to say to him being the introverted, shy, socially awkward gal that I am. I thanked him for signing my *Carry On* CD cover and asked to take his picture. Seven years later that picture still hangs in my cube, at work. Meeting him is and will always be one of my favorite moments in life. I wish I would have wished him a happy birthday, as it was in four days, and found words to express my gratitude for him and his art and had profound questions to ask him.

I didn't know Chris personally but it feels as if we knew each other intimately due to a common life long battle with depression. His words weave through the very depths of my soul and help me know myself, as well as feel less alone. His voice and lyrics conjures up feelings in me I didn't even know existed and comforts me like no other. I am sorry he succumbed to the oppressive beast but he valiantly fought for so long and so hard and helped so many in the process. He is now at peace.

Chris will always be my favorite singer songwriter. I am forever grateful I was able to see him live, six times. I am forever grateful to him for sharing his soul through his esoteric songwriting and leaving so much great music. I am forever thankful I lived in the universe at the same time as him. I will forever miss him. Chris took a piece of my soul with him and forever embedded a piece of his within mine.

Mickey Horvath Gombosi

I had gone to a concert in 2011 in Allentown, PA. I screamed out "I love you Chris" and he responded "I love you too!" Then after the show a large black SUV came bolting down the alleyway I was walking down. I shot them the finger and realized it was CC!!! I told my boyfriend "I wish he would've hit me cause then I would have seen Chris." He is such a humble man!

Mike Harrington

Chris was a great, kind-hearted soul. Our son, Tony Harrington, is the kid that built and gifted Chris the custom chopper bicycle that Chris featured on his Songbook tour. They have been friends since Tony was nine years old and Chris always made time to see Tony when in town performing at shows. His thoughtfulness and kindness will never be forgotten. Our thoughts are with his family in this time of loss.

It all started in 2011, when Tony built a tribute chopper of his favorite artists, the bike had a big sculpture of Chris Cornell's autograph on the rear fender and a home made tank with hand painted Soundgarden, Audioslave, and Temple Of The Dog art work. Tony was nine years old at this point. When Chris first saw the bike he couldn't believe it. Tony said he had a vision for the bike, when people saw the bike from the back they could look through the sculpture of his autograph and see the real thing on the tank. He asked ever so politely if Chris would do that for him. Chris said "Tony, I would be honoured". He put "to Tony you rule" and that was the start of an amazing friendship.

So as a few years past Tony started to out grow the bike and he decided that he would like to gift it to Cornell for him and his kids to enjoy. When Tony made contact, Chris said he was blown away and would love to have the bike. So after they meet, Chris rides it out on stage and shares the story of Tony's gift. What happened next was unreal as Chris decided to use the chopper at every show and share the story of friendship and kindness. The last time Tony saw Chris was last year at a concert when Chris called Tony out from the audience to come up on stage and share a few moments.

Cornell was a very kind hearted soul and will be missed greatly.

BY THE FANS AND FRIENDS OF CHRIS CORNELL

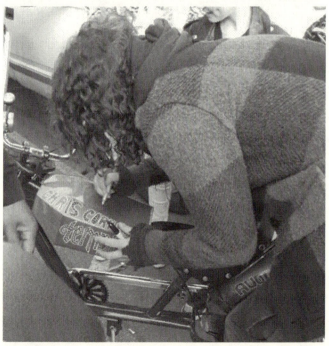

BY THE FANS AND FRIENDS OF CHRIS CORNELL

Miriam Maiorano

This sense of loss inside me won't leave me alone. I feel incomplete and don't know how to thank Chris in the best way I can. He showed me what singing really means and I'll be grateful to him till the end of my life. He's my biggest inspiration and he will forever be. We've lost an incredible artist he touched the souls of many with his voice. Now he's gone and a piece of us is with him now, wherever he is.

Rest in peace, Chris.

Monica M. Rosales

Thank you from the deepest levels of my being for everything you gave to us, Chris. You were a bright light in the darkness for many of us giving so much of yourself to the world through your music and lyrics. You had a singular way of saying things we all felt in such a beautiful way and your voice was so full of soul and emotion that it resonates still with people all over the world. Your works will continue to inspire and comfort people for all time. We love you.

Monica M. Rosales, Austin, Texas.

Myra Baucum

I'm still at a loss for words, but this is the most together thought. It doesn't come close to saying it all...

For the spark that ignited a fire in my soul 23 years ago, inspired me to create pictures of sound, and guided me through the darkest hours and years. You are loved and missed.

Nairi Sargsyan

Last two weeks I read many posts by people about their experience as fans Chris Cornell and Soundgarden. I found out about Soundgarden in 2009. I was a huge fan of Nirvana then. I must say that I wasn't listening to SG or Audioslave so much, but I knew that he's one of the greatest legends of grunge. The next year I fell in love with Alice in Chains. One of my fave songs was "Right Turn". Cornell's voice kills me there. Last year was the year of Pearl Jam. Then somehow I found "Mailman". I was going through a break up and that ONE song helped indescribably. BUT still I wasn't into SG's or CC's music... until this March... I don't even remember why or how I started to listen to Chris Cornell. That was the darkest moment of my life. I have fought against depression for many years and I hate to say that I tried to commit suicide twice. But this year was even worse.

At one point I felt that I couldn't handle it anymore and... I found THAT music. I was going through hell. For some personal reasons I felt terrible both at home and at the office. I could not talk to my friends because I couldn't trust them. The only thing that I had was Chris Cornell's music, both Soundgarden and Audioslave. Three songs were like oxygen for me. "Show Me How To Live", "I Am The Highway", and

"Be Yourself". Especially the last one - I was repeating it again and again - "don't lose any sleep tonight, I'm sure everything will end up alright' I cant even tell you what his words mean to me.

I remember talking to my colleague while discussing *The Promise* (I am Armenian so the movie means a lot to us) I said "you have no idea what kind of legend wrote a song for the film". She looked at me like I was going crazy.

Anyway, I started to feel better recently. So I thought that it's time to know better the musician who saved my life. So I got as many songs as I could that day and went to work. I remember I opened my Facebook page – saw his photo and number 52 above. I couldn't understand what was going on. He's gone.

Since then I can't listen to anyone else. I have been listening one album after another since that damned day.

People including my friends don't understand why I feel so bad these days because of "just a rock star who died many, many miles away". They don't understand: his music was the only thing that I had when they failed to be there for me and when I was completely alone. I still can't concentrate on my daily work and I can't believe he does not exist anymore. At the same time, I blame myself because I know that his family and friends are dealing with the real pain and I have no right consider his loss my pain. And there are those of you who started to listen to him since the 1980s or 1990's. You saw him live and I couldn't even dream about him. I can only imagine what you feel now. These thoughts don't help. I feel terrible pain.

Sorry for writing so much but there is something else that I'd like to say. Some people say that Chris Cornell's music is depressing and sometimes with signs of suicidal thoughts. He's not depressing to me at all. Yes, he writes about depression (because he is dealing with it), sadness, loneliness but his music is always hopeful. It helps us to hold on, do not give up. Yeah life sucks but it's alright, everything is going to be fine – I put it in very simple words but isn't the real message of his songs?

They make us stronger. He cares for people and makes them feel happier.

And about his death. I hate myself for reading about the details of his death. It feels disrespectful. But I really need an answer... why? how? I feel like the catastrophe was born just in a few hours. Maybe we will never know the Higher Truth.

I am listening to *Euphoria Morning* right now. "There is a space now and forever empty because of that. It's never going to make sense. It's never going to feel right. And it's always going to hurt". JC

P.S I refuse to talk about him using past tense.

Nancy Jane Bragg

Thank you for everything Chris! The world will never be the same without you!

Narene Russell

On Chris's Higher Truth Tour in Australia I was lucky enough to score front row V.I.P seats with my young son. A month or so before the concert Chris had an 'Ask me any Question ' on his Facebook page. My Question wasn't really a question but a request. I told him my son was a huge fan as was I and told him which concert we'd be at and where we were sitting. I just asked if he could wave at my son. Well he didn't reply to my comment but he did answer other people's, which was awesome.

Fast forward to the concert and we took our place front row, so excited to be there. When Chris finally came out on stage he scanned the crowd and made a beeline to my son. He bent down and smiled the most beautiful smile and waved at him and I just mouthed "thank you". No sound would come out, I was so shocked. Shocked that he'd even read my request but more shocked he'd remembered it. What a kind beautiful man to give us that memory to keep. I'm eternally grateful.

Rest in peace Chris. You had a beautiful heart and you will be missed so much by so many. My thoughts and prayers are with your family and friends xxxxxxxxxx

THANK YOU: A TRIBUTE TO CHRIS CORNELL

Photo: Piera Alessio

Nathan Wesley

I Know Your Name
A Song for Chris Cornell

The sea under a moon
A haunting open night
The highway for my
Rolling wheels to ride

Your words resounding of
The sweetest euphoria
A voice so strong
Oh how I long
To hear you sing your song

The day I tried to live
Your tune upon my head
To drown the fear and ease
A troubled heart to rest

THANK YOU: A TRIBUTE TO CHRIS CORNELL

A soul of the loudest love
You outshine a thousand suns
A voice so strong
Oh how I long
To hear you sing your song

And here we fall
On the blackest yet of days
Your time has come
But we will always know your name
I know your name

As riot leaves the mind
A burdened hand lets go
May you rest in peace and find
A higher truth to hold

Though your candle has burned out
You say hello to heaven now
A voice so strong
Oh how I long
To hear you sing your song

As seasons roll away
And body turns to dust
The man of golden words
Forever sings in us

Nathaniel Rawiri

You were my Lennon and McCartney rolled into one. That voice, those lyrics, the bands, them riffs. From the first time I heard you, I knew you would be a huge influence on my life and music some 25 years later. Thank you Chris for giving me enough music to last a lifetime, the memories of some 20 live shows to always remember. I will be forever in your debt... See you in Olympus my friend.

Nathaniel Rawiri
(New Zealand)

Nicole Finch

I want to thank you Chris for giving us the gift of your music and your amazing voice. You showed that you can be amazingly talented but still be humble and kind with a heart of gold. Rest now and find peace. You are missed, but not forgotten, and forever loved.

Nina K.

BEAUTIFUL HEART AND SOUL

Your heart and eyes spoke to me,
- I saw the beauty within you.
Your soul touched me,
- your lyrics and voice let me see the secrets within.
Your eyes glow and shine with pure light and love.
- you're such a beautiful, sensitive, humble heart and soul.

In your presence and in your lyrics, you always captivated us.
In your presence there is calmness, happiness and love.
Your perfect, steady, strong, hard, amazing voice is the most powerful voice of all.

Your heart and eyes spoke to me,
- I saw the beauty within you.
Your soul touched me,
- your lyrics and voice let me see the secrets within.

THANK YOU: A TRIBUTE TO CHRIS CORNELL

Your eyes glow and shine with pure light and love.
- you're such a beautiful, sensitive, humble heart and soul.

You're a man fearless, you could do any song and you make it your own.
You're a radiant beautiful, multitalented, unique man.
Your beauty, charisma, passion, intelligence and knowledge so deep.
Your beautiful smile, eyes, laughter and humor.
You were a man with deep compassion.

Your heart and eyes spoke to me,
- I saw the beauty within you.
Your soul touched me,
- your lyrics and voice let me see the secrets within.
Your eyes glow and shine with pure light and love.
- you're such a beautiful, sensitive, humble heart and soul.

Your light will never fade away.
Your words will always carry on.
You will never be forgotten.
You will forever live on.
You will never be outshined.

Your soul belongs to our creator.
You were a traveller, a borrowed human with skin and bones, a unique beautiful heart and soul.
Thank you for all you did and will always do and be for all of us.
Thank you for your beautiful heart and soul and your music, for being YOU.
I LOVE U, WE LOVE U and miss you forever, our beautiful heart and soul, Chris Cornell.

Patty De Michele-Insigne

Chris, you were just a guy from Seattle who happened to have some amazing vocals, and then you busted out to become the "King of the Grunge". Your musical talents were huge far beyond what you expected, but you continued to make music and became a lead singer of three major bands. WOW! Musicians loved you, fans adored you and even Hollywood wanted your songs. However, you were just this humble guy who loved to sing and write songs. I don't think you ever knew how AMAZING you were. There will never be another singer like you.

I am so grateful that I have lived in your era and was able to see you play live. Ten times doesn't seem like enough now, but it has to. I never got the opportunity to meet you in person to tell you thank you for your music and to tell you how your songs have inspired me when times were bad. Thank you, Chris for all your amazing songs and your beautiful vocals. You have gone too soon but I sure hope you are at peace now, rest easy and fly high with your wings.

Paul Stensrud

In May of 2009, my oldest son and I saw Chris for the second time at the House of Blues in downtown Disney in Anaheim (yeah, I raised my son right... his first two concerts were Chris Cornell).

The show was great and at the end of the show he and his bandmates were throwing picks to the crowd. A guy in the audience had brought his son who appeared to be about seven or eight and was on his dad's shoulders, and Chris got a drumstick from the drummer (I caught the other one!) and walked over to hand the drumstick to the kid. As he did this a total douchebag in the crowd reached up and grabbed it for himself.

However, Chris never let go of the stick so what ensued was a tug-o-war between Chris and the idiot trying to hijack the kids stick for about ten seconds. I was pulling at the guys arm and yelling at him "He wants the kid to have it!" Chris finally won the tug-o-war and made sure the kid got the drumstick. He could have just given up but he didn't, he was determined to give the kid the stick. I always hoped he knew I was on his side and helping the kid get the stick since I already had one, and a couple picks to boot.

Pete Thorn

November 20, 2007. Backstage somewhere, Chris threw the knife from the deli tray at the door and it stuck. He was very stoked and proud, I had to snap a pic. I assigned the picture to him in iPhone contacts, so it'd pop up if he called - made me laugh every single time. He was many things, and one of them was FUN. Very. Miss you man, so much.

Piera Alessio & Mary Chiodo Jennings

Doesn't Remind Me...

We were lucky enough to have seen Chris Cornell four times in 2015, the last time on December 11th, at the Sydney Opera House.

What's Tom Morello got to do with this? Roll back to the Springsteen High Hopes Tour of 2014 here in Australia. Tom guested on that tour and that reminded us to delve back into his catalogue.

Enter - revisited Audioslave. First, the self titled album, blast out "Like A Stone", "I Am the Highway" and "Show Me How to Live". *That voice.* That led to us being on high alert for any Chris Cornell tours. In the meantime we played some Audioslave bell music here at school.

Fast forward to 2015, and the announcement that Soundgarden were playing at the Soundwave festivals. Despite thinking we wouldn't last the distance at an all day festival, the promise of Chris Cornell live was too good to pass up. Tickets were purchased for Melbourne. Two of our students were desperate to see another band at Soundwave so the deal was we would sell them our tickets if we could still see Soundgarden somewhere else. A sideshow at Festival Hall was announced and we secured tickets - the deal was done.

A pleasant February night had us entering Festival Hall, Melbourne. In the past this venue was used for wrestling matches but was also a good grungy music venue. Soundgarden went off that night! Chris was in fine voice and had some interaction with the exuberant crowd. We enjoyed the setlist and couldn't believe we were finally seeing him live! After the show we got stuck at the merch bar and were later ushered out by security as a large part of the crowd had already gone. We were on a natural high and discussing the sweaty sexiness of Chris, when we found ourselves exiting via the loading dock where the band's transport was waiting for them. We saw Kim waiting to get into his van and just as we "thought" we'd hang around until someone asks us to leave… out comes a freshly showered Chris and, with a smile and a wave, he gets in the van.

Later that year *Higher Truth* was released and with that came a world tour, luckily including Australia. With hearts in our mouths we attempted to purchase tickets for the two Melbourne shows, with a friend helping us with Sydney tickets. Result - three for three, and front row centre stage each time! Leading up to the shows we familiarised ourselves with as much of his back catalogue as possible and discovered and rediscovered his music.

Show 1 at the Palais Theatre Melbourne, 4th December 2015: As we sat in our seats we realised we were going to be within arm's reach of Chris and those boots! He wandered on stage without any fanfare, picked up his guitar and mesmerised the crowd. His voice seeped into our every pore and made a connection. It sounds like a cliché but we felt like he was just singing to us. It could have been because we gave him a standing ovation before he even started! He acknowledged it with "Thank you nice ladies". At the end of the night he only shook four hands – and we were two of them. We were lucky enough to say "thank you" and to look into those beautiful blue eyes. There was a strict no photos policy those two nights.

Show 2 at the Palais Theatre Melbourne, 5th December 2015: – was the very next night and we were there again – same spot. It has to be said that there is something to being that close to an artist – you hang on to every word, action and strum of guitar. You can see them taking a breath, thinking about the next song and interacting with their fans.

As teachers we can't usually take days off to attend concerts. However, the Sydney show at the Opera House called us to make an exception and now looking back we are very glad we did. The Opera House was a perfect venue for that four-octave voice. He walked nonchalantly on stage and once again mesmerised us. Remember this was our third show in six days, front row centre mic, so there was a good chance that he was starting to recognise us. He started singing "Doesn't Remind Me" as he strolled like a wandering minstrel towards us. This is when we threw caution to the wind and thought "Fuck it!" Piera caught his eye and gave him a little cautious wave and Chris acknowledged it with a smile. Since he was looking directly at us Mary blew him a kiss to which he raised his eyebrows and smiled! We know this actually happened because the woman next to us leaned over and commented "That's impressive!" And it bloody was. Except that we never thought it would be our last interaction with him.

We are glad that our one year with Chris Cornell was so memorable and so personal. Always in our heart.

(For more photos, see pages 26, 85, 223 and 301.)

THANK YOU: A TRIBUTE TO CHRIS CORNELL

11 December 2015 – Sydney

R. Scott Mattingly

The news that Chris Cornell died hit me like a proverbial ton of bricks. I feel a little silly reflecting on a celebrity death in this way as if I have some close, personal connection to the person. Truthfully though, Chris Cornell was, for me, an example of the power of resonant music to move a person. Of course in high school, I went through the standard grunge rock phase with all of my friends and Soundgarden was a key part of that. I loved the rockers in their catalog and I was devastated when the band originally broke up. As it happened during my senior year of high school, perhaps it felt a bit like the end of an era for me personally as well. The thought of untapped potential has always been a particularly frightening one for me; I've long felt an intense desire to make ongoing progress in meaningful work. I could never fathom how a good band couldn't just make it work for the sake of the music and of whatever message(s) they might be trying to send. And yet, perhaps it was how things were supposed to be, the evolution of a vocalist working toward being an artist.

During my freshman year of college, I took a first-year seminar on the topic of Etymology. For the final paper, I needed to analyze the history of a word(s) in a manner that exposed deeper meaning. I was struggling to find a topic that felt personal enough to me, worthy of writing about for the requisite ten pages. On a short drive, I listened to "Sunshower" and was struck by the beauty of the song, especially the lyrics that managed to be overwhelmingly uplifting without being the slightest bit disingenuous. It was exactly what I needed to hear at that moment. I had my topic... I would analyze the impact of music on society by examining the etymology of the word, "music." And it wasn't long after that when I first heard his cover of "Ave Maria". It felt like he was growing up and maturing just as I was. Whereas Soundgarden had been an excuse for me to jump around and yell at the top of my lungs with no particular purpose other than perhaps to work out some teenage angst, this was something new and good. My awkward teenage years were moving into a more peaceful phase and I was growing in my faith, just as his music and lyrics seemed to shift.

Fast forward to April 4, 2009: I had submitted ten interview questions for a radio contest and was selected to interview Chris. That night, I spent twenty minutes talking with him and he couldn't have been nicer or more authentic. Perhaps ironically, halfway through, he spoke candidly about death and the impact it could have on his children. When it was over, he complimented my interview with surprising sincerity. Then, he introduced me to his wife, Vicky, as if I were someone important or a friend that she just had to meet. It was an incredible, unforgettable experience.

And so now, as I reflect on all of these memories, I'm sad about the stunted potential of a dynamic vocalist and songwriter, as well as of a husband and father. Still, I have hope in the resurrection, and I know that the work he has done will continue to have a positive impact on his children and on the many people who have been impacted by his music just as profoundly as I have been.

Rachel Dunay Joseph

Took my kids to the Higher Truth Concert. We had seventh row, center. We were so close that we saw Vicky and Toni sitting on the sage to the side of Chris. The performance was flawless. Seeing him that close was a dream. Hearing him sing all of those beautiful songs that he wrote as well as the covers was just amazing! I had seen Songbook and Soundgarden previously with my husband and taken my kids to see Soundgarden, but this was my favorite show because all four of us were witnessing this magic together as a family so up close and personal. I will love everything Chris Cornell forever and ever.

Rachelle Kanuch

I saw Chris twice in Lakewood, Ohio for his acoustic tour. His voice is mesmerizing. Not very many men give me goosebumps singing, but he did.

After hearing it was a suicide it killed a piece of my heart. I battle with depression and my ex didn't believe depression is real. I had to email my ex make it a point for him to SEE that. It's sad that it's taking so many wonderful dying for simple-minded people to realize depression and suicide affect even the best. How many more do we need to lose before people start to understand and accept depression as being a REAL PROBLEM!!!!

Chris you always be in my heart. I love you, your voice, your music and your heart.

Rebecca Meadows

My first reaction:
!! My favorite artist has passed away at 52 ?!!
CHRIS CORNELL WAS AN AMAZING SONGWRITER WITH A LEGENDARY VOICE.

You could feel his soul reverberate with such raw strength and clarity - he could do everything from soulful, soft, acoustic serenades, to screeching rock hard vocals, to his album with Timbaland, *Scream*, which you can move to (danceable) - and mastered it all. I loved covering his songs due to his blues-like thralls.

His lyrics, unlike most, are more akin to poetry - not mainstream, not your typical stuff.

He was truly versatile and his music, a gift to this earth. I only love singers who I feel are truly artists (not just mainstream) and Chris is the one I respect the most (Josh Homme is second).

I have been listening since high school.

I only had a chance to see him twice, but deeply hoped for many more.

Regina Keehfuss

During one of three shows during the Songbook Tour, in AC, NJ, I yelled out, "I LOVE YOU!!!" Turns out, Chris had it put on his Songbook CD. It's the first line in "Can't Change Me" before Chris talks about writing the song.

During my 27th show, at The Scottish Rite Theater, Chris had his back to us, picking out a guitar, and I called out with all my heart and soul, "I LOVE YOU, CHRIS!" He turned and walked to the mic and smiled and said, "I LOVE YOU, TOO!"

So many other stories and meetings and discussions on legalizing cannabis during a SG show at the Tower Theater in Upper Darby, PA. Busting on us for smoking in the pit. Turned on the lights and all. Lol. It was awesome.

Peace.

Rhonda Bates

I can put in to words what every single song he has sung has done for me, helped me feel pain, love, has brought me out of bad times, through my depression, built me up. Sooo many lyrics are what I have felt but couldn't find the words myself... I am truly heartbroken. Better go put on some CHRIS, so he can sing to ME.

Rhonda Giannasi

Thanks for keeping me feeling something, Chris. Like you, my sister took her life too, and I'm not mad at you two anymore.

Signed OUTSHINED.

Robert Brooks

I discovered Chris's music from the video game Road Rash in 1994 after the *Superunknown* album was released. The first song I heard from Soundgarden was "Outshined". When I first heard that song I thought it was Pearl Jam, then heard "Rusty Cage" and "Superunknown". Then I love all these songs. Finally I heard "Black Hole Sun" on MTV when it played. Then in January of 1995 I heard "Fell on Black Days". I fell in love with that song. Then I eventually brought *Superunknown* and then looked for *Down On The Upside*. I did want to see them back in 1996 but was not able to and they broke up a few months later. I was devastated.

Chris' voice and lyrics with Soundgarden was so inspiring. Their music, as well the other Seattle bands, have got me to pick up the guitar and start playing. I was nervous that I didn't hear any new music from Chris until the great *Euphoria Morning* came out. That was and still is masterpiece and Chris's best solo work. I also a few years discovered Temple of the Dog. That music inspired me too. "Say Hello to Heaven" and "Hunger Strike" were great. Then Chris formed Audioslave and did like the first album by them.

Finally by 2005 I saw Chris performed for the time with Audioslave. I didn't come to just hear Audioslave songs. I was happy that Soundgarden and Temple of the Dog songs were included. I love his solo acoustic performance of "Black Hole Sun". The solo acoustic performance soon became legendary. After Audioslave broke Chris released two solo albums before the Soundgarden. I wasn't too wild about *Carry On* and did strongly dislike *Scream*.

When Soundgarden reunited my first thought I have to see these guys. Finally in the summer 2011 I got to see Soundgarden not once but twice with in a week. I saw them in Newark and Philly. Both of those were the best concerts I ever went to. If I did ever met Chris, the answer is no, but he did acknowledge me. That felt so great.

His music was what kept me sane. I struggled with my own demons. When Chris became sober many years before he inspired me to get sober. At some point I stopped going to shows. I kept looking forward to new music, whether it will be Soundgarden, solo, Temple of the Dog or Audioslave. Unfortunately, I couldn't attend the Temple of the Dog show because I have been going through my personal demons and plus my mom was dying from cancer. I lost my mom on December 7 this past year. I have been grieving all of it since. Then I went to rehab this past May to overcome my addiction.

On the morning May 18 of this year, someone from rehab told me Chris passed away. I was saying no way then I saw it on Fox TV. I was shocked and completely heartbroken. I wanted to AMA out of rehab so I could numb myself. I heard it was a suicide and that shocked me. I know he had periods of depression but I was in disbelief that he would kill himself. I got more information when I came home. I just didn't stop listening to his music since I have been back. Now in my opinion I don't think Chris killed himself, but I am not going into at all. That is something I rather keep private. This is all about honoring Chris's legacy. At some point I want to form a tribute band to honor the greatest singer in our time. So RIP Chris and thanks for the wonderful music.

Rochelle Weinard

Chris Cornell has been the voice of my life. He's been there through trauma, love and my sobriety. I've had a hard time listening since he left but am slowly coming around. His music will always be the soundtrack to my life. Our world will never be the same without him, we've lost a beautiful soul. My heart aches for his family and all of his fans. I will be forever grateful to have lived in his time. I'll always love Chris Cornell.

Loud love ~ Rochelle Weinard

Rocio Alvarez

BY THE FANS AND FRIENDS OF CHRIS CORNELL

THANK YOU: A TRIBUTE TO CHRIS CORNELL

BY THE FANS AND FRIENDS OF CHRIS CORNELL

Ron Cameron

No one has captured the moods I feel better than Chris Cornell, I have been listening to him for 32 years to date. I listen to him when I'm up, and when I'm down. I first saw him in '96 when my wife was 6 months pregnant with our first born. That's her behind me in the photo. She's 21 now.

Ron Hunt

So... let's share some good memories and talk about some good times y'all have had because of Chris Cornell. I'd love to read about them and smile a bit thinking about all the good times and great music we've had because of him and his talent.

For me... it was the early '90s and things were all flannel and hiking boots. I was just learning to whitewater kayak and those early days of beginner swims at the river were fuelled by Chris' voice singing those great songs. I'd fling that flannel shirt around me and lace up those hiking boots, and drive toward the river with Soundgarden booming loud. Funny thing is, I still have my old drivers license from that time and in that pic there I am... rocking that old flannel. Ha!!! I found those old licenses a while back when I went to see Soundgarden in concert in 2013 at The Riviera Theatre in Chicago and I just had to snap a cool pic of my old Soundgarden cassettes along with my old license and the tix... good memories.

Anywho... back to the river. I was lucky enough to be able to pull my Jeep riiiiight next to this awesome surfing wave at the river and learn to surf it in my kayak while "My Wave" was playing in the background... it was awesome!!! Perfect song for that!!! I'd take a few swims here and there, collect my floating gear, swim up to the shore, sit on the riverbank next to my

Jeep, and rest while listening to that amazing album. Then I'd go for it again... rinse and repeat. I swear I swam a thousand times on that river!!! There I'd be going down the river backwards or upside down in my first kayak, a purple/black/blue/white multicolored boat that I sooo loved and still have to this day. Upside down or backwards... but always with those good lyrics and music in my head. As time went on I learned to kayak kinda, sorta good and traveled all over the US to boat some pretty mean rivers... and in all that traveling the soundtrack to those roadtrips and my crazy kayaking adventures was always Chris' amazing voice... whether it was in Soundgarden, Audioslave, or his solo work... his lyrics and voice was just what I needed to get through all those dangerous rivers. That was well over twenty years ago since I began kayaking and Soundgarden's album *Superunknown* came out... times have changed now. I've changed boats a dozen times. My skills improved a bit. I'm often far away from my vehicle, boating through remote canyons so I'm not sitting as often beside my vehicle listening to music and paddling easier water... but I have never ever stopped listening to his music while boating!!! Now I take a waterproof case with waterproof earphones attached to it and my MP3 player, iPod, or iPhone listening to big booming music as I run those big booming rivers in my kayak... and to this day Chris' music is still my go to soundtrack for all these continuing reckless whitewater adventures. Thank you Chris... thank you for always being there at the river with me. :')

RIP Chris Cornell... lead singer of my favorite band ever.

Just about five years ago, I went with my cousin Waylon and saw Soundgarden perform in the tiny antiquated concert hall The Riviera Theatre in Chicago. IT WAS AMAZING!!! Waylon had seen them perform several times before and told me after the show, "You'll never see another Soundgarden concert that great!!! THEY ROCKED!!!" ... indeed, they did. Chris' voice was perfect, the darkly lit venue was charged with electricity, the small club vibe of The Riviera Theatre had the feel of times long past of the Seattle Grunge scene, the band charged forward harder through each song, there was stage diving by Chris, old songs as well as new were screamed out in that signature high pitched voice of his, there was my favorite band tearing it up... and there we were right up front!!!

We will never know what demons one has inside them...

one man's heaven is another man's nightmare. Chris Cornell fought with depression all his life and from that fight he wrote some amazing songs... "Fell On Black Days", "Just Like Suicide", "Black Hole Sun", "Burden In My Hand", and many others laced with dark thoughts and depressive undertones. I've heard many say that suicide is a coward's way out. No... it's definitely not that. I can't imagine the nerve, determination, courage as well as the emptiness and desperation, that one must have to gather in order to complete that last sad solemn task... but the last thing I think of suicide is a coward's way out for it is not. For whatever reason... whatever battle they are fighting... they are struggling and have lost their way and feel that they are out of options as well as just helping their family out by not burdening them any longer... indeed, often their last thoughts are of that very thing... no longer burdening their friends and family and loved ones. They are not being selfish. They believe that they are better off no longer around family and friends and, while longing for a connection or help... just drift away until they can see no one there for them... even when everyone is right there reaching for them.

Chris wrote the song "Fell On Black Days"... with his

passing those lyrics now mean more than ever to me. I've had my far share of 'Black Days' and that's what I call them when I get depressed because of that song... I'm so sorry that you couldn't find the light during your last Black Days Chris...

I will miss you. I will miss your songs. I will miss your words and lyrics. I will miss your voice.

Thank you Chris Cornell for bringing great music into my life.

Farewell Chris... now, with your passing, I've fell on... black days.

My cousin Waylon called me with the terrible news early that morning. When he called and said, "I've got some bad news about Soundgarden." my heart sank... I knew what it was. I just sit back and tried to remember every moment of that wonderful concert in Chicago, as well as sadly realizing that I'd never see them play together again... and have been bummed out ever since.

His music touched us all. He played the soundtrack to every roadtrip that I've ever went on. I play his music when I whitewater kayak down raging rivers through waterproof headphones. It's just the music and lyrics that I need for things like that... it's just the music and lyrics that have touched my heart and soul perfectly.

Farewell Chris... truly we have fell on... black days.

Rory Jennings

Friends,

The weight of losing our beloved Chris is so painful and leaves a scar across our skies.
His arms around the world have brought us all together to drown in our grief.
Take comfort in the fact that throughout human history, we were alive during his sunshower and bathed in the Majesty of his genius.
We have lost a friend, but his timeless beauty brings comfort throughout the seasons. His music lives on in all of us, he is never truly long gone.
When we asked for light, he set himself on fire.
Peace & Love.

I remember Chris being so funny on his Songbook tour in London 2012. He spoke a bit about most of the songs he was performing, and just before going into one from *Scream*, he told us all how Timbaland came to his house to kidnap him and force him to make the album! What a guy!

Rose Hurt

I waited in line on February 15th at the Wiltern for eight hours to be on range 1 to see Soundgarden. I made this shirt while waiting in line. Threw it up on stage. He thanked me for it and put the shirt on for the whole encore. I'm from North Dakota.

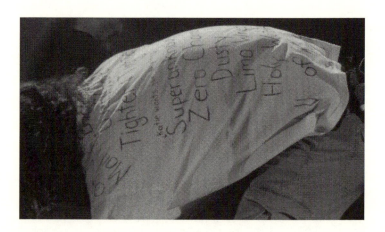

THANK YOU: A TRIBUTE TO CHRIS CORNELL

BY THE FANS AND FRIENDS OF CHRIS CORNELL

Rose-Lea Otten-Sadowski

My son and I were invited to meet Chris by his family. It was my son's first show ever and I am so glad it was Chris. Chris was graceful and humble and seemed intrigued with my son's love of his music and spent a good ten minutes talking with us. I also got to meet Vicky and his daughter Toni. This was the night she performed with him on stage in NYC at the Beacon Theater, 10/19/15.

My son keeps his picture on his desk, and mine is on my night table right next to where I lay my head each night. It's there with all of the other pictures I treasure... and see first thing I see when I awake and last before I go to sleep. We will miss him for the rest of our lives.

Ryan Gavalier

When I look at Soundgarden and think of a truly rocking song, this one pops in mind ["Slaves and Bulldozers"]. On top of awesome work by all of the instruments, Cornell's vocals were extremely brutal, and they put chills on me. This was one of the songs that made me fall in love with the band years ago, and it still affects me the same now. As I listened to it again yesterday (along with many other songs), I was just realizing how much I miss Chris. I never met him or saw him live, but he truly had the greatest voice ever, and it's so sad to think that no one will sing like him anymore.

I remember the first time I head Soundgarden. It was somewhere around five or six years ago, and I was going through the CDs that my dad gave me, and I found *Badmotorfinger*. I put it in and "Rusty Cage" started. I was so blown away by the unique sound that I just had to listen through that whole album. After that I saw he had *Superunknown*, and I listened to it too. I was impressed greatly by both albums, and was instantly a fan of the band. There were great riffs/performances by every member of the band, but what I noticed most of all was the brilliant voice of Chris Cornell. He had such a distinct voice that tore through songs, but there was also a certain beauty to every word he sang. As I grew older, I listened to his music from his solo career and Audioslave also, and I couldn't find anything I really disliked. Whether it was his original songs or covers, he made them special with the undeniable talent that he possessed.

Hearing that Cornell passed away hit me hard, because even though they aren't my all-time favorite band, or even one I listen to every day, but they were the best of that era, and extremely special to me too. He was such a talented man, and he seemed like a genuinely nice person too. Losing him is such a major hit to the music community, because honestly he had the voice that everyone wishes they had.

Sacha McGowan

Charleston, SC, June 19th, 2016. "No concert will ever top this experience " I told my husband after the show that night. I was right, no show will EVER compare. Thanks Chris for allowing me on the almost 30 year journey of poetic mastery!

Sam Harris

Rather than mourn his loss, I'm going to celebrate his life. I've started watching old videos of him, listening to Soundgarden, Audioslave, Temple Of The Dog, and his solo albums back to back. Me and my brother are going to smoke a doobie and just jam the whole of *Superunknown*.

He was an amazing, amazing, man. Inspired me to sing and songwriter and the only singer I have cried for.

He will be missed. But let's all celebrate his life rather than be upset.

Samantha Lynn

I remember walking down the halls of my high school with my headphones blaring Soundgarden and thinking wow, this guy understands me. Chris has been my favorite artist since I was 15... I'm 24 now.

There were so many times when I felt that his music was all I had to live for in my life. His dark, brooding lyrics, his soul-warming voice, and music took me to another place when I couldn't deal with life. I've never felt such a connection to another artist. Through depression... then later addiction... and then recently recovery from addiction... Which brings back the depression... the only person who's been steadily there through all that is Chris.

I feel like I lost a part of myself. A few weeks before he passed away, I started going on a binge of his music again. Watching YouTube live performances, interviews. Reading articles. Seeing how we've struggled with the same kinds of things. I honestly don't think I'd be here if Chris didn't ever exist. I'll always fall back on his music. I feel like I knew him almost, it's weird. Like I connected with his soul. He made such a positive impact on my life... and always will.

Rest In Peace Chris.

Samarra Black

Chris was my hidden angel, my protective and dark angel. He was there, through his music, through his incredibly beautiful voice which was able to pierce your own soul so deeply to soothe a bit your suffering, your pain, and to fill you with joy, a so obvious and natural joy, in all the high and low times of your life. Reflecting your own disarray toward a life, it's difficult to find a meaning except through love.

I can't imagine a world without him. I won't. I know his music will always play an essential part in my life, until the end. Sadness, deep sadness. Shocked, because it was a sudden death and it's like I had lost a close friend, someone who helped me when I was down, who made me happy when I danced and sang with him in a concert hall. So happy then... I can't explain what you feel when you really love music and you recognize just the first chords of a song... an intense shiver penetrates your whole body... A so wonderful feeling... Only few men can let such a footprint in your heart, in the world, reaching the narrow circle of those who really changed something and made the world a better place to be. No one sings like him anymore.

Since his death, it seems as if I was living a real nightmare. I can't imagine what he felt during his late moments alive. I prefer to remember his smile, his generosity toward people he didn't even know but he changed life through his sound, making it more bearable, more meaningful, more beautiful. Softer. And he did so paradoxically with a hard, dark and heavy sound – grunge one - and a voice sometimes full of rage and despair.

Eternally regretted and admired... as true artists should be. Love him forever, with all my broken heart. Love his music for years and it will never change. Since his death, I can't listen to other bands. I need his voice, his music, not to admit what happened because I can't but... But that's all I have now... and I should add, fortunately: lots of people we love who disappear, and leave just a big hole in our heart and memories in our mind, but he let us so more. He gave us that incredible musical legacy and I promise I will always protect it and help to spread it all over the world.

For weeks now, I'm in mourning. Since I learnt of Chris' death, I feel terribly sad all the time. I can't stop listening to his music again and again as if I was refusing that atrocious reality, as if it was the only way to say goodbye and to say how important he was to me. For hours, I was denying but I read all that articles and all that posts that confirmed he has gone and I had to confront that ugly truth. Nevertheless, I'm still denying... I can't imagine he will not compose and sing and play music anymore, I can't bear the fact that I'll never see him on stage anymore. Nothing can fill the emptiness I feel. It's difficult to find the right words cause it's already a way to put away that terrible loss and I can't put away anything. It's difficult to find the words cause words are too weak to express what he embodied to me. I'm deeply shocked. Now, I felt totally alone again and the wonderful lyrics of "Like A Stone" are turning in a loop in my head... Each little word today can remind me his words as if my own life found its echo in his lyrics.

Obviously, I couldn't say all that embodied his voice to me, since the first time I heard it live in 1992 in France, Vincennes, on Guns N' Roses tour. I remember the discovery of grunge in the early 90's with the release of *Singles* at the movie theatre and its fantastic soundtrack... When you enter that musical world, that sound, that voice, you can't be the same anymore. To me it was a fantastic shock, a great revelation. It was MY sound. And when Cobain died, when grunge's wave retreated, I felt closer and closer to that music.

I followed Cornell's career with Audioslave (Zenith, Paris, 2005) and then alone (Showcase, Paris, 2007; La Cigale, Paris, 2009 ; Trianon, Paris 2012 and 2016) but I was so enthusiastic when I heard Soundgarden has reunited... First, I saw videos of the Seattle and Lollapalooza concerts and I thought, "he's got long hair and a guitar again, Soundgarden's really back!" Than I wondered, "wow, I'll be able to see them on stage again" and it was a beautiful memory (Belgium and France 2012, Luxembourg 2014).

As if I grew with him by my side, not like a friendly shadow but like a real and helpful friend who carried me through life cause I went far in self-destruction - and I still do - but I'm still alive... as would intensely say his great friend Eddie. I know I was really lucky to have been able to see him several beautiful times but I don't feel so. Now my heart is totally broken. I know I will not recover... It's not enough, it will never be: each time I went out of one of his concerts I thought "wow ! Want to see him again" and now I know I will never see him on stage again. I just have those marvellous memories in me forever. All of them are wonderful but I'd like to detail some particularly. So even if to see him during the explosion of grunge was great, I think it's always difficult not to be the main band on stage cause the crowd is not totally with you...

So 1.) Audioslave, 2005: I have been really impressed by his voice (and his height too!). That's the first thing you discover in live, the beauty, the depth, the intensity of a voice. Those

years I listened a lot to Audioslave who carried a lot of intense emotions to me, who walled me back a man loved and lost, so I was very enthusiastic. The band was really solid. Even if he was only singing at that time and left his guitar to one side, Tom was really wonderful. Such a way and energy to play guitar! They were incredible.

2) Chris, 2007. A wonderful concert in a very small concert hall, which had just opened in Paris, near the river. With Audioslave he used to sing also some Rage and Soundgarden songs, but in 2007 it was all his own repertoire. I can't say how happy I was when someone asked him for "Say Hello to Heaven" and he sang it, such an emotion... Temple Of The Dog is a masterpiece to me and it was the first time I listened to it live. He also sang "Call Me a Dog", a fantastic one, for his baby who was in the concert hall.

3) The Soundgarden show I saw in Luxembourg was the best I ever saw of the band. They played songs from *King Animal* and ancient stuff. It was really, really wonderful. Dancing and singing a lot and I can say living a concert from such a great band is really a very happy time, a real release.

4) Songbook tour, 2012... I think the best show I've ever seen of Chris and maybe the best show of my life and I have seen a lot... All his repertory and lots of covers of artists and bands he loved... but what was really incredible, besides his beautiful voice which can carry so many emotions and which resounds deeply in me as if it was love and pain in raw state... so what was really incredible was his presence on stage. And looking at him you just thought, yes, here is a great artist, nothing superfluous. No need for lightning, or other musicians, just his voice and his guitar. The scenery was very simple, just a circle of guitars behind him, some objects and a bar chair. It was totally enough and yes, it feels as if we were at a bar with a good friend. He spoke with us with such a simplicity and ease... And he spoke a lot, explaining sometimes the origin of a song, telling a good story etc. His family was there, just at a side of the stage... And his voice. I love it with strong guitars and battery behind, oh yes I do cause I love that

kind of energy, of violence and of sound, but during the acoustic tour you could surely confront better with his extraordinary voice...

Remembering all those beautiful times fills me with joy and pain at the same time... No, I couldn't say all that embodied his voice to me. Music, I would say real music, music made with heart, talent and all your soul, can carry so much emotion and memories... I loved while listening to his voice, I cried as well... His voice seemed to answer me, reflecting my joy and my pain, resounding in me again and again, carrying me in certain states of grace or accompanying my descents into hell. I recognize myself in his lyrics, in his sound and It helps yes, it helps so much not to feel totally alone and stranger to that world. As if it was like me, with my strengths and my faults. It's just the magic, the strength of creation, no doubt, to go beyond what one expresses and to be able to move, upset, disrupt... other sensitivities. Maybe it was just a way to transcend his own depression, I don't know, but it resounds very deeply in me.

Chris had this power, this beauty, this incredible charisma when he spoke with the crowd with such a friendliness and simplicity... This charisma radiated from him... I was lucky enough to see him several times on stage and to be each time close to him... I can't forget that energy, that beauty, that voice... It seemed to bear both the rage of an era - that of the grunge - and the depth, the emotion, the passions and the sufferings of a remarkable being. His music and lyrics took other meanings now, and that's what happened for main works of art.

He may have told all he had to say and thought it was time for him to go but I don't think so. A true artist as him was able to reinvent himself, to call himself on question again and again and to push the limits to create something you didn't expect. But I deeply respect his choice cause I understand his suffering through mine, and because I loved him. Vain. All my words sound so vain to me trying to say how essential he was. Vain cause I'd like to say nice things about him cause he deserves that but the fact is that if he was in my life, I wasn't in his own so I just can talk about my own experiment with his music and meeting him live. I couldn't say he saved my life because I don't feel I am, I'm still struggling every day and I don't know if I will not give up the fight one day too. But his lyrics, his music, make me fight until that day.

Even though I'm deeply grateful to him for all the meaning he gave to my life, cause sharing your own feelings through art, whatever the medium you use, painting, music, sculpture etc., telling others they are not alone with their joys and pains, that's a real gift of love. His voice is life to me, as if all his soul and his heart were in it. He helped me to survive and I don't know how I can get over his death now. Of course he left us a fantastic musical legacy but nothing can replace his beautiful and intense presence in the world, nothing can replace the wonderful feelings we shared listening to and watching him live and above all alive. Rest in peace Chris, you gave us so much, and that gift, your music, your voice, what you were, remain forever. Thank you so much for everything, for your unique and talented music, for the man you were in that world, generous, simple and so friendly. Oh God I'm so sad....

Loud and eternal love.

Samarra, from Paris.

Samuel Fiunte Matarredona

There are no Exit Wounds

There is a continuity through my life, you can call it a river, a road or any other visual image that conjures a continuing picture that leads you back to where you come from and further to where you are going. Now that continuity is broken, the way has come to an end and the fall is never going to stop, or to stop hurting.

Chris Cornell was, for me, the person who shaped me. That is a tall order, but a real one. He was the guy whom I look up to try (and fail miserably) to model my looks. He had long curly hair? I tried that (too bad my hair was growing in afro style). He cut his hair and wear it straight? I tried that (too bad there was no way to get my hair straight) etc. I was obviously looking up to an impossible, his looks had no match, but I tried nonetheless. I'm sure many others tried too. He was a role model in other ways: Talking about being reclusive on his teen years, or having social issues and singing and writing about those moments when you don't feel great definitely had a weight on me. All those are things I recognised in myself, and the fact that other people could sing that to me, reach out to me, was a way of getting through that and finding myself.

Obviously it was not just him. Soundgarden were and are a 4-way machine and they all had their importance. And so did other bands, and other things that influenced me. But Cornell was there first and foremost.

The news of his death brought me flashbacks of the day I heard Soundgarden were to break up in 1997: I got it from a friend, couldn't believe it at first, ran to the internet to check it out (in 1997 in a little town in the north of Spain that meant skip school to go to one of the few computer shops that "sold" internet time, while right now I just took out my phone and scrolled Twitter). The anxiety in both cases was the same. I had reverted to be a nervous teen scared of this to be true. And it was true. Only that this time it was forever.

I begrudged Cornell for breaking up Soundgarden. The same way he epitomised everything that was cool with the band, he epitomised everything that was uncool in the post-Soundgarden world. It was totally stupid, but that feeling was there. I had *a* Chris Cornell in my head, and I argued with him many, many times over the years. About the break up, about his solo career, about joining with ex-RATM, about his RnB album. All I wanted, as the little kid that I was inside, was to go back, go back to Soundgarden. And he gave that to us in 2010. And everything was right in the world then.

The previous bit is just to show how silly I was. I learned a lot of stuff in the last couple of days that do not match my previous idea of Cornell… because I never worried about knowing more than what I had in my head. And I regret that very much.

Since I was 14 I have interwoven Cornell in my life in countless ways. One example: because Cornell's lyrics for Soundgarden were hypnotic, I decided to try to translate those to understand him better. That led me to think I knew enough English that I could move to the UK (I was so wrong about that), and because I moved to the UK I learned enough English to eventually find a job in my current career, which has nothing to do with what I studied. He did that. He put me on the path I am today.

I need to share one more of those: Because Cornell had a fork necklace and my mother knew how much I loved Soundgarden, she suggested that I could have one too and my dad did it for me. I still have it, and I still wear it. It is a secret language between Soundgarden fans, and at the same time is a secret language within my life. It ties my mother, my father, Cornell and me. I bled over that necklace; I cried when I thought I lost it when I travelled to Paris to see Audioslave; I have fought with custom agents over the fact that it looked like a weapon and I had to dispose of it… now both my mother and Cornell are gone and that necklace is going to be a constant reminder of that, the same way as if I had it stabbing me. But that is a pain that I welcome, that I will carry on and don't want it to be gone. That is a pain I don't want an exit wound from.

Cornell is a figure for the ages. He is going to stay as he was, not gonna age. But he was also a figure on my life, and I am going to have to carry on walking alone. And that hurts very deeply, in ways that are hard to put in words. This has been my sorry attempt.

I never really knew you, but I wish the best to everyone who did and who will miss the real you: your family and friends. And to everyone who felt they knew you through your music and art. You are gone and I don't mind why. Rest in peace in the Superunknown, Chris.

Scott Browne

Scott Kvasni

I just took the lyrics from "The Day I Tried to Live" out of my FB bio a couple weeks ago, after it had been there for four or five years. Still think it's one of the most profound songs ever, lyrically.

This one hit me really hard and people might think I'm crazy but I feel like this guy was a modern day prophet. He was blessed with inhuman abilities and wrote just the absolute greatest lyrics. Relatable on the surface, accompanied with a lingering message.

His voice was perfect. Scientifically it was outstanding because he could reach four octaves but more importantly, emotionally it was stunning because the man knew when to hold back and when to go hard. And when he went hard he hit notes with a signature shriek and unparalleled ferocity. It was the perfect voice from a beautiful soul.

Personal story - got to see him at the Sound Academy by the docks a few years ago. For those familiar with the venue, you know it is an intimate setting. This was nothing like when I was lucky enough to see them play at the Molson Amphitheater, which is too big to capture the same vibe. There's no bad seat in the house at Sound Academy and we were right beside him. I could see the beads of sweat on his face. The torment and anguish in his performance, when he got to those dark songs. The ones from *Superunknown* and *Badmotorfinger*.

At one point mid-concert he just stood still between songs. He wasn't moving or saying anything. Just standing there with his eyes closed. You could sense his deep focus and the suspense and anticipation was mounting in the crowd. We were loud and rowdy at first, then an eerie hush. At this moment my friend leaned over to me and said "Cornell is looking pretty God-like right now." Not to sound blasphemous but he was right. His presence was ominous. No sooner did my bud finish speaking when Chris looked up and the band burst into "Jesus Christ Pose". For years this had been a track I thought was just okay. Sometimes I even skipped it when I listened to the BMF album. But since that moment on, it has been my favourite Cornell song and arguably my favourite song of all time! The performance was incredible. I can only describe it as a spiritual journey. His voice was so piercing, and when he got to the "like I need to be saved" line... Dear Lord. I'll never forget it, and the album recording does not quite match the intensity of that performance. I'll never forget him shrieking "Saved!" repeatedly, and I've thought about it often over the past few years.

I could go on and on about other stories about Chris and how he influenced me, as I'm sure he touched a lot of you, but I just wanted to share that one.

Thanks Chris for everything, you will be missed but I will always cherish you. So grateful that this world had you to spread your message of love and acknowledge the dark side of humanity in such a profound and unique way.

Sean May

Thank you Chris. You changed me for the better.

Sean May.

Shane McIntire

Within an Echo of the Soul: A Tribute to and Personal Reflection of Chris Cornell

The theatre went quiet, just before a spotlight shone down, as if God himself had chosen and he stood before us. Tall, lanky, full bearded, Chris Cornell stood on the stage, holding a guitar. The theatre erupted into a mass of cheers and applause. And as Cornell launched into an acoustic rendition of "Scar on the Sky", the crowd went silent once more. His voice rang out, echoing through the hall and we were awestruck. We were witnessing a God at work. But I noticed something else that I never noticed about him before that, when I only ever saw him on late night television and YouTube...

Depression is, undoubtedly, the bond that links Chris Cornell and his fans.

It is almost eleven years ago at this writing that I first discovered the music of Chris Cornell and yet it feels an eternity. I can recall the precise moment I first became enamored with his music. I was twelve years old, and the first Daniel Craig James Bond 007 film *Casino Royale* (2006) had just released in theatres across the world.

The film opens with a particularly brutal fight followed by the introductory credits, over which the film's main theme, "You Know My Name", is played. That was my introduction to Cornell's art. The film was outstanding and Craig gave a stellar, gut-wrenching performance as Bond, but I didn't leave the theatre that day thinking about the film. It was the voice that had echoed throughout the theatre that captivated me most.

Something in Cornell's voice struck me someplace deep. I knew I needed to hear more. The next song I discovered an acoustic rendition of "Black Hole Sun". That was that.

Within a month, I explored most of Soundgarden's catalogue and Audioslave was next up.

It wasn't long before teenage me thought of myself as an expert on all things Cornell, and not a day has passed since that I haven't listened to his music. Middle school, high school, familial deaths and depression, yet his music remained. It still does.

Fast-forward eleven years.

I was drifting off the night I opened my phone to check my Facebook one last time before sleep. The first item I saw in my news feed was from CNN.

Chris Cornell was dead at 52.

From there, I don't even know where to begin.

Chris Cornell's music meant more to me than any words can possibly describe. I discovered him at twelve and his voice was there for me in a way that nothing else was. I went through middle school, and high school and he was there for me. In my time of need, his voice was the one thing I could count on continuously. My grandmother and my grandfather were like parents to me, and as they passed, one by one, into the next world, Chris Cornell remained.

My Grandmother passed on when I was sixteen and my grandfather checked out when I was twenty-one. When my Grandmother crossed that divide, my Grandfather and I stayed up most of the night with *Temple of the Dog* flowing through the speakers of a phonograph somewhere in the darkened room.

When my Grandfather passed, I carried on the ritual. *Alone.*

For reasons that are obvious, "Say Hello 2 Heaven" is particularly close to my heart.

Now I find myself once more removing the *Temple of the Dog* record from its sleeve, and taking it for a spin. The night I heard of his passing, I got physically ill and honestly, I haven't slept well since.

Someone once referred to his voice as an "echo of the soul" and while I do not know who said that, it is as close as anyone can come to describing him.

I only ever saw Chris Cornell perform once. It was the Keswick Theatre in Glenside, Pennsylvania on April 10, 2011. Times were better then and my grandfather was still with us… But I also remember times when Chris Cornell's music was the only thing that could get me through the day.

Sometimes it still is.

The only live performance I witnessed was beyond comprehension. 27 songs over two and half hours. No backups, no bands, just a man, a guitar and a voice. That memory will forever live with me, just as his music will continue to guide me through the dark times, inspire me to do my best and continue to be help me find the light.

Even as a writer, I have trouble finding the words to describe his presence in my life. His voice, that *echo of the soul*, the understanding of it all, and his dark, poetic lyricism have all been there through the years.

In short, his music is always playing when I write and is always omnipresent in the darkened corridors of my own memory palace.

With Cornell's guiding voice, I wrote a novel last summer and recently, I have started another. This one, with great admiration, will be dedicated to him. After all, it should be, as it is a novel about and allegorical of depression. *That great, untameable beast lurking the shadows, waiting to get the better of us.*

Ultimately, this is why I believe we all connect with him and why I believe referring to his voice as the aforementioned *echo of the soul* is the most appropriate way to refer to him. Chris is an echo of all of our souls. And for those of us who suffer depression, the music is more relatable and accessible then to those who don't have to deal with it. It spoke to us, became a part of us, as he understood in that unique way we all did. His voice and poetic words said the things our hearts were feeling. And when he died, a part of us died with him.

It is never not going to hurt hearing his voice from now on.
And in the end, all I can say is thank you Chris.
And Rest in Peace.

Cornell was all alone up there, standing in the darkness of the stage with only one light shining down from above. He was alone in a roomful of people. Like anyone who lives with the beast. Only for a moment, I felt his eyes caught mine. But for that one moment, I felt closer to him than anyone I ever knew before or since. The music that spoke of darkness and depression, of Black Days and Seasons gone by connected us, as it did with all of your fans…

No one sings like you anymore.

Shanida Carter

I heard Soundgarden had reunited and was going to play the Prudential Center in Newark a few months after my first daughter was born in 2011. I hadn't listened to their music since I was a teen consuming everything grunge. That concert was amazing. Chris' voice sounded as powerful and as clear as the album!

I couldn't find my Soundgarden CDs so I went to FYE and picked up *Badmotorfinger* and *Superunknown* to get reacquainted. I listened every now and then until March 11, 2014. I had a miscarriage and spent the whole night in the hospital alone. My husband had to stay home with our sleeping toddler...

I went into a deep depression. Lots of praying. Lots of tears. I popped in *Superunknown* soon after and listened to it everyday, ad nauseam, for months. It was on to, from, and at work... while I was in the shower... while I cleaned the house... basically every time my daughter wasn't around because I turned it up loud...

A few months later, I was pregnant again, and gave birth to my precious son. I named him (Chris)tian. Chris Cornell's voice and that album got me through one of the darkest times in my adult life. Of course, I had my husband and daughter and close friends and family, but those songs, especially

"Fourth of July" and "Just Like Suicide", took my mind to places that I didn't have to go in real life. It helped me get some clarity about the ugliness of life and how we just have to deal with it and soldier on...

I was at work at my TV station when the wire came across that Chris had passed. It was as if someone punched me in the heart and stepped on it. I was hoping that I would get the chance to tell him in person how he helped save me. I will be forever grateful to him and Soundgarden. I hope this very short version of events will bring his family and other fans some comfort knowing he made a real difference in life, especially mine.

Sharon Edwards

Dear Chris and family,

As a long time fan I simply say:

It takes a very unique, special artist to have a big impact on the world. The beauty of music transcends generations, reaches out to hearts and minds of all kinds. Music is the voice of the soul. It expresses what cannot be said and which is impossible to be silent. We remember a place in time, good times rocking out at live concerts, rushing out to buy new tunes, lazing back and relaxing to your tunes. Tunes that lift our days and console us all in hard times. Tunes speak a different language. These are gifts that we as fans have received and from such a unique artist as you, Chris Cornell. I'm very thankful for this.

I was a member of the Australian Cornell Street Team and was lucky enough to receive VIP tickets to a Melbourne show and a meet and greet back in 2008. A special night with great memories. I was lucky I met Chris, who came across as a humble, gentle soul. Bless you, Chris, and thank you.

Chris, your legacy will live on forever in your tunes.

To family and loved ones – my deepest condolences in such a devastating time.

THANK YOU: A TRIBUTE TO CHRIS CORNELL

God bless and watch over you all \m/

Sharon Edwards
South Australia

Shubhang Joshi

Dear Chris, thank you. I first heard you in "Be Yourself" and instantly fell in love with your lyrics and your voice. I just knew it then itself that you were special, at least to me! You have carried me through my pains, the toughest moments in my life. While Soundgarden nursed my wounds, Audioslave helped me get my spirits up.

You're a poet, a lover, an amazing singer and a lovely person deep down. I haven't met you but I can feel your soul through your words - 'these pages of phrases'. I used to tell my friends that if God could grant me one wish then it would simply be to have your voice. It's the most beautiful voice I've heard. There's a prayer in every scream, a kiss in every howl. Only you could pen such lyrics and sing them. It was my dream to listen to you live. Unfortunately, it was never to be.

I don't know if you took your own life, whether you did it consciously or not. All I know is that you must have given life to a lot of people who really needed it. I love you Chris. You have made me cry, laugh reminisce, love, persevere. And you shall continue to do so. You've made me live Chris.

Thank You. Rest In Peace.

Stephanie Gordon

I can't remember exactly when it was, but my first exposure to Soundgarden was seeing the video for "Rusty Cage" and I was hooked. I was 14 at the time and all my friends had crushes on Anthony Kiedis or Eddie Vedder. Not me. I loved the music and had a girl crush on the lead singer Chris Cornell. He was like a wailing dark angel that reminded me of a devious pirate captain, haha.

My first time seeing Soundgarden live was at the Stabler Arena in Pennsylvania in 1994. It was the best gaddamn rockin' show hands down. I shoved my way to the front and was getting crushed by all these sweaty guys moshing by me, but I didn't care. It was a once in a lifetime experience. I didn't get to see them live when I was in the Army, but the songs definitely kept me sane during basic training and multiple deployments. I remember being so pissed I couldn't get Audioslave tickets when they came to Philly! Then in 2007 I snagged tickets for my boyfriend, now husband, to see Chris solo at the Croc Rock, in Allentown. It was such a small and intimate venue. Chris sounded so great that night.

Other shows I saw was Projekt Revolution in 2008, (he sang with Chester from Linkin Park on "Crawling" and "Hunger Strike"), solo at the Electric Factory 2009,

Soundgarden reunion tour 2011 in Philly, the MMRQ 2013, and Temple of the Dog Philly the first night. All were great shows. I've been to a lot of rock shows and nothing compared to seeing Chris live.

His music has gotten me through some rough times. Just a few months ago when I was prepping for an interview I was listening to "Be Yourself" to pump me up. I ended up killing it and got the new job. I've listened to Soundgarden, Audioslave, solo work, or Temple of the Dog almost every day for 26 years. His passing has cast a shadow on my household and left a void in my soul. I don't think I will ever truly come to grips with what has happened.

Chris, I hope you knew how much you were loved! This wasn't supposed to be the ending of your book.

Peace and love, Stephanie Gordon.

Stephanie Mackley

Yours was the voice that will forever be embedded in history. Like many others, you were and are apart of the soundtrack of my life.

My last memorable concert was with you, in October 2014 at The Bridge School Benefit in Mountain View, California, with your good buddy and brother Ed Vedder. The moment I got those tickets I prayed that you both would sing together, then I had the grandiose hope that it would be a Temple of The Dog song. The day came and that very moment I heard the strum of "Hunger Strike" begin time stood still. Everything was in slow motion, and at that same time my heart skipped a beat and the tears of joy began streaming down my face. I was crying so much I couldn't sing along... what a blubbering mess I was.

I am proud to have been apart of your journey as a fan. You elevated music forever. I will say again what I had requested be written on a note and placed onto your stone...

'Chris, My heart hurts, but I know you are always around in spirit. Thank you, from the bottom of my heart, for your beautiful gift that you shared with the world. Let your soul be free and at peace. Stephanie Mackley - San Jose, California.'

Stephanie Munoz

Chris Cornell wrote and performed songs about trouble and loss better than any other artist I'd ever seen or heard before. He'd certainly experienced his share of loss at an early age and the songs he wrote could touch my emotions in ways that I didn't even know was possible. And of course, a lot of it was in his delivery of the song performances. That voice, it seemed impossible that it was so perfect, so full of emotion, a seemingly unearthly range, with howls that could shake your inner soul. Truly, Chris Cornell had the most amazing musical instrument that I've ever had the privilege to witness hearing live, that incredible voice.

In the early 2000's, I was busy trying to become a mom with my new husband. Then trouble and loss started to rear its ugly head. My roommate before I married and good friend, Rita, died of ovarian cancer at the age of 46. Another good friend in Austin had met the man of her dreams, married him, gotten pregnant and then found out she had breast cancer. She had the baby and was dead within three years. She was 43, her name was Kristi. This wasn't supposed to be happening, friends in their 40's dying of cancer. My husband Arthur and I were struggling with infertility for four years during that time, which was completely devastating but we finally decided to adopt two kids. Life was hectic but good again, even though I didn't get to see Audioslave live because of new mom duty. Soundgarden had broken up the month we got married in April of 1997, and I was so disappointed that I hadn't got to see them before they were no more.

Time moved on - another friend who had also struggled with infertility and was in my mom support group also died from cancer after having her two sons, this time it was Hodgkin's lymphoma. The sadness that I felt was crushing, so many young amazing women dying before their time. Then was the year of Hurricane Katrina. God, what a horrible year that was. My mother lost her home in Biloxi, MS, and came to live with us in Houston. She and I were struggling with PTSD and depression. My husband lost his job of 26 years and fell into deep depression with us. Times of trouble were upon us. I had been listening online to Chris's *Unplugged in Sweden* after that over and over. Those songs and his voice spoke to the depth of sadness I was experiencing. During his Carry On tour in 2007, I had joined his Street Team, and had won a meet and greet, after already meeting him during the tour at least two other times. He was so gracious to the fans during those meet and greets. He made us so happy. I would request songs at the shows with signs, and he would perform them and talk to me and the audience about them. He performed the song "Wide Awake" about Hurricane Katrina when I requested it with a sign at the Seattle show at the Paramount that year. Here is what I wrote about Chris and *Unplugged in Sweden* during that tour:

"I think about when I first heard the *Unplugged in Sweden* concert - the unhappiness I felt was more than I had felt at one time since being an adult. The weight of the world, I knew the mundane reality of what that meant and it had shackled me. After I listened to that concert, I felt completely different. "Redemption Song" gave me hope. "Peace, Love and Understanding" reminded me that those are the things that I needed to hang on to the most. "Thank You" made me realize that I was still loved. "Wide Awake" made me cry for all that was lost for me and Mom in August of 2005, but also that we are not alone in our loss, and that others had lost far more and that the hurt caused by those events would continue to be felt for a long time. And that it was ok to be angry about it. "Doesn't Remind Me" made me realize that I could mourn my losses but that it was ok not to keep mourning them when I was ready. "Billie Jean" made me think that just because something was done before, doesn't mean it can't be done again in the present, with more emotion, more passion than it was done the first time. "Like A Stone" had me thinking that the people depending on me could also be depended upon for my well-being. "Fell on Black Days" reminded me of the dark days we had experienced together and that change is the thing that can ultimately make our family whole again. "Original Fire" made me realize that it is good to remember the past, but to still embrace the present. "All Night Thing" spoke of warm nights I'd had and a lot more warm nights to come and that being warm with someone you love is much better than not having that.

The whole concert made me feel again in ways that had just become numb. It amazes me that even today, eight months later, I remember feeling every one of those emotions listening to those songs. Then I realized that I had to hear those songs played live, not just for entertainment value, which usually was enough for me being a music fan, and a longtime Chris Cornell fan, but because hearing them performed by the artist himself would make those emotions even more real for me. Experiencing the emotions again while Chris was pouring his emotion into them while performing was necessary for me in validating that they were important to feel. I didn't know at that time just how much my senses had been deadened and beaten down into despair, leaving me empty and bereft of really being able to experience life as I had before the hurricane.

So, somehow I have to tell him all of that. When he played "Wide Awake" for me, all of those emotions I had came flooding back, this time with a great sense of closure, like the shaman had just given me the aha answer to the greatest question in the universe. Every emotion I had had for the last two years plus was completely validated and the joy I felt knowing that I could freely move on from that chapter of my life was overwhelming. So of course, I cried. Definitely tears of joy. And then Chris thanked me for reminding him of the song. Well, thank you, Chris, for reminding me to live. Maybe now he will understand why I keep requesting "Thank You" at every show..."

Chris's tour that year helped me with the absolute worst time in my life and made 2007 the best year of my life. After that year, Chris kept putting out albums and going on tour, and I kept going to his shows. I met so many amazing people that have become my friends for life. I had the most amazing times, traveled all over the U.S. and Canada, waited in line for hours with my friends to get to be at the rail and have those special experiences that Chris made sure the fans got. He shook our hands, fist-bumped with us, let us touch his guitar, let my friends play guitar with him on stage, let me sing "Ty Cobb" into his microphone ("hard-headed, *uck you all"), signed all of our memorabilia, wore shirts that we gave him, played all of our song requests, talked to us, smiled and laughed with us, crowd-surfed on top of us, even poured his sweat out on us from stage and at the rail. That was some good sweat. He was so giving to the fans. It was so incredible.

Then things got even better when Soundgarden reunited in 2010. Then we not only got Chris solo, we got the amazing Soundgarden tours and new Soundgarden music. It was like we'd died and gone to heaven early. I won a lottery on Soundgardenworld.com to go the intimate Vic show in Chicago before the big Lollapalooza redo where Chris joked "We've played Lolla thousands of times before, but it's good to be back!" Chris also started the Songbook tours in 2010 and we got the Chris that intimately shared every emotion he'd ever had with that amazing voice again. The tributes he did to Jeff

Buckley and Natasha Schneider were so special. The red phone that Jeff's mom gave him in case Jeff called from heaven, the turntable where he spun Natasha's version of "When I'm Down", these were special moments. I cried at every show, tears of joy, tears of sorrow, tears of thankfulness to be hearing that voice at that time with those people.

Chris continued to get better and better at his acoustic shows and the ones that he performed on the Higher Truth tour he sounded better than ever. That year, again I was recovering from tragedy as my best friend from childhood had succumbed to brain cancer. Then my mom died. I was sad again and Chris again had the perfect songs to help synthesize with and then overcome the sadness. Plus he was doing more and more covers and they always seemed to be better than the originals in pretty much all cases. The shows were pure gold. I kept going back again and again. I am so glad I did. I was beginning to heal from the grief of my best friend and mom passing. And then came 2017.

This April I was ecstatic that Soundgarden was again touring. My husband Arthur and I celebrated our 20th wedding anniversary at a show in Tampa. I had made plans to see them again at Rock on the Range and then in Houston and in Dallas. Usually, Soundgarden and Chris did what I called the "Texas Trifecta" and would do shows in Houston, Dallas, and Austin when they came and I would go to all of them. I was a pretty spoiled rotten super-fan. Thank you, Chris. But Tampa was my last show. The unfathomable had happened. My favorite guy was dead. I had been having a moment of guilt when planning the Houston show because my 14-year-old daughter was going on an orchestra field trip and I wanted to be a chaperone, but my co-worker, who is also a Chris fan, said to me "Go see Soundgarden. You don't know how long they'll be around." I took his advice and bought the tickets, although it didn't take much to sway me to do that. Little did I know, his words turned out to be prophetic in a way that has devastated me and all the fans I know. To know Chris was to love him. This kind of loss may never be felt again in the rock world. He is irreplaceable. Until I see you again, Chris, thank you for all you've brought to my life with your amazing music, angelic voice, poetic vision, and humble and kind soul.

Your music, the songs
Your heavenly voice
Your humor, your smile
Your warmth, your humbleness
Your loneliness, your holiness
Your emotion, your devotion
Your fans, my friends
Things I will miss more than seems humanly possible.
Thank you for sharing so much with us in this life.
See you when we all say hello to heaven, our sweet Chris.

Stephanie Munoz, Houston, TX.

Stephanie Silva

1996. Darkest time of my life. I heard "Fell On Black Days" and couldn't believe someone was actually speaking to my soul. I can't explain the peace that his words and music gave me, I fell in love with Chris Cornell that day. My heart hurts because of his death but I'm grateful for the beauty and love that I personally carry with me everyday because of the music he gave to me! You will always be my #1, CC.

Your loving and forever friend and fan, Stephanie Silva.

Stephen Coppola

It's almost 1am and I can't sleep. I wanted to share a story real quick.

I had left for deployment in August of 2013. It was going smooth for a couple of months but stuff was starting to get to me. There was this guy that I wasn't getting along with (forced to be in the same place with people can get messy sometimes) and we had an argument. I had been up for two days straight and so had he, if not longer. I couldn't sleep even though I worked all day and he had to come in for the night shift. We were both so ridiculously tired and I decided I wasn't going to bed. I had brought my guitar and decided I was gonna learn "Seasons"... he was playing his Xbox while I sat in the corner of our little box we worked in.

At some point in time, he took off his headphones and we sat there and learned how to play that song together. He helped me with the melody while I figured out how to play this beautiful song. I never quite nailed it like I wanted, but I remember it was an all night thing and the morning crew came walking in and we both had lost track of what time or place we were in. It's one of those memories I can't seem to get out of my head. The music made these two people connect even though we hated each other.

He's still my friend to this day and it's because of a shared love of music. So, thank you Chris. Sorry for the rant, but I wanted to tell that story because it's one of the highlights of that time in my life. Much love guys.

Sue Ann VanGilder

Such a difficult day. I just tweeted one last time to our Chris. I've been repeating what I tweeted out loud all night long in case his soul is still around. Then, in the few hours of sleep I got, I dreamt of him.

To Chris : You are so very loved! It's alright. Everything is alright. Be in peace.

Susan B. Harty

Music has always been an important part of my life. My dreams even have soundtracks, so I think of my favourite musicians as my unseen friends. As an artist, Chris Cornell was an amazing singer, a great rhythm guitarist, but an incredible songwriter.

He could take a friend's challenge of a cassette case with five song titles written as a goof and create powerful songs like "Spoonman". He could evoke smiles from the best moments of being in love or allow you to find solace in a saviour rescuing child soldiers. His lyrics could be cryptic or deeply personal.

The true skill of a great songwriter is when they write something that feels like it came from within you. During my best and worst times, his music has joined me. He wrote with sorrow, regret, compassion, anger, and joy, and when I felt those things or needed relief from them, his music was and is there for me.

His family is heartbroken; my heart aches for them, and for myself. We never met but I feel like I lost an old friend who was taken from us decades too soon.

Sylvia Lee

Chris Cornell was not just a rock singer, or some tragic talent from the rainy Pacific North-West. Chris Cornell was a Father, a Son, a Husband, a Brother, an Uncle, and a Friend. Chris was talented and witty and genuine and above all, by all accounts of those who knew him, a good person in a world that seems to be getting more and more questionable at times.

I think after all the musical tributes are done and the pain of his leaving begins to numb - the best way that we, as people who claim to love the man with the golden voice from Seattle, we can honor his life, is to reach down and pick up those who are not doing as well as we are - or share what we have with someone who needs it and show loud love in all we do.

Chris did leave us with some amazing music... videos that give us glimpses of his wit and insights on a number of subjects and himself... and he also left us with an example of what it means to be one of those "good people". Say hello to heaven for us Chris... 'til we meet again.... Loud Love.

From the ZRockR Magazine article "Reflections on the Life and Legacy of Chris Cornell..." by Sylvia Lee, Editor in Chief, ZRockR Magazine, Las Vegas, Nevada.

Tamara Ann

Chris I grew up listening to you. Every song you ever made, will be forever, deeply ingrained in my cell memory. You were pure light and love, one in 7 billion. I know God graciously welcomed you to heaven because you lived a life full of compassion for others, you were void of ego and everything you said was meaningful and purposeful. A wonderful friend and role model for many.

Your light (soul) shined so bright, you're now a beautiful knight, shining bright up in the stars now. Your not being here on this planet has left many with tears, enough to fill an ocean. Your kindness and talent was/is a gift to this very troubled planet. Thank you for raising my vibration through your music.

Lots of love forever and always, Tamara Ann, MI.

Taryn Lee Thompson

I have been a fan of Chris Cornell since 11 years old and now I am 35. My first CD I ever owned was Temple of the Dog. Surprisingly, I understood his darkness at way too young. "Hunger Strike" and "Say Hello to Heaven" really changed my life.

I had always wanted to see him live, it was definitely on the top of my bucket list. Finally on August 21st, 2014 in San Diego I got to see Soundgarden for my first time. I brought my 13 year old son with me, which was his first concert ever. I'm so glad I got to experience that with him.

Thank you CC for your huge contribution to my love of music, and I will be blasting it until I take my last breath!!!!

~Taryn Lee

Terri Parks

Dearest Chris,

When I first heard you sing back in 1989, it was immediately love at first sound. And for the following 28 years, you have been a constant part of my life.

I thank you for giving me your voice and your words to listen to over and over again. I will always take comfort in that.

I thank you for the countless concerts I was so very fortunate to attend.

I thank you for being so kind and humble when I met you for the first time in 1999 and to be different, I had you sign a personal check of mine, which you said was a first, and you happily obliged by making it out to yourself for a million dollars. We both had a laugh and to this day it still makes me giggle when I see it.

Then in 2003, I went to a meet and greet and brought my ginormous, shirtless poster of you to sign for me, wherein I jokingly apologized for bringing such a "sexy" picture but told you it was in fact, my favorite. Again, we had a laugh and you graciously obliged.

I will never, ever, forget the mark you left on me and I promise to honor your memory for as long as I shall live on

this earth.
 Much Love,
 Terri P. Las Vegas, NV, USA.

Tessa Jamerson

To my CC, people tell me I should be a writer but I seem to only write well when it's something I'm passionate about... so here ya go!

A bright light forever gone and a beautiful but troubled soul at peace. A glorious voice silenced well before its time. You fought until fighting became too much. You were strong until being strong wasn't enough. You tried to speak to us through song but all we heard was music. People think that this world was just too much for you but you were too much for this world. You gave us pieces of yourself and forgot to keep anything for you. The holes left were too deep for you to fill. How could we not see the pain? How could we not feel the hurt?

Many of us seemed to forget the man behind the voice, the scared, fragile human being behind the guitar and for that we have failed you. We now see what we all missed after it is too late. We demanded all of you and being the man you were you never hesitated to deliver no matter the cost to you and again we are sorry. The love and admiration we gave you was only a bandaid for the gaping hole in your soul and once it came loose you couldn't stop the flood so you fixed with the only option left to you. You untied your hands!

THANK YOU: A TRIBUTE TO CHRIS CORNELL

You accomplished so much in three decades and while we feel you had so much more to give, you were done. We as true fans don't care how or why you are gone, we only feel deep antagonizing pain over the fact that you are truly gone and that we can't wake up from a never ending nightmare. The number of lives you've touched and saved definitely lined your path to heaven and we all know you are waiting on that grand stage, guitar in hand to sing for us once more...

BY THE FANS AND FRIENDS OF CHRIS CORNELL

Chris Cornell
With thanks to Tessa Jamerson for the photo edit
JAN 16, 2015

 Chris Cornell ✓
Chris has asked us to pass on his thanks, **Tessa Jamerson**. - Team CC
Jan 16 at 2:50 PM • Unlike • 👍 72

 Tessa Jamerson
Wow! I can barely breath I'm so happy! Tell him he is so very welcome! I am glad he liked it! You made this girl's day for sure!!!

THANK YOU: A TRIBUTE TO CHRIS CORNELL

Tiffany Brook Meyer

We traveled different paths but I always felt connected when I heard you.

The years, when the music was my most important. Then, the music had to move over to let my recovery be first. It worked for me and it seemed to work for you. Each allowing the other to grow.

Then came family. How could all three fit together? You showed me how.

This triangle of love, spirit and wisdom has flourished with each side feeding each other. I share your music with my children to further strengthen the triangle.

Now you are gone, leaving an incredible legacy and vast emptiness. Because I did not know you personally, I know that soon I will only smile when I see your pictures or hear your voice, though it hurts very badly right now. My hope is that someday, your family can do the same.

Peace,
Tiffany in Seattle.

Tiffany Van Drimlen

Thank you Chris Cornell for EVERYTHING! Words cannot express how your voice held so many together who would have otherwise fallen apart. Thank you!

Tina Arvanites Dumont

I started off with a poem... Robert Frost... nothing gold can stay... leading to nothing which is perfect and beautiful can last forever, but I am really grateful to have grown up with his music and all the good times it evokes, that it seems only proper to THANK him. Right?

So here goes: Thank You for the soundtrack of the happiest years of my life. Thank You for that voice like no other. Thank You for that beautiful smile and head of hair. You are so loved Chris. We are all so broken you are gone. Rest Easy. You will NEVER be forgotten.

Tina Brown

My Dearest Chris, I can't believe I'm writing these words to you after just less than a year ago my dreams came true during a week that I always regarded as HELL and then became my *Euphoria Mourning*. July 6 and 8th I spent some time with you. I only wanted to "Thank you" for your timeless poetic music that helped heal my soul, after losing my Robbie at nine months old in July 3, 2012.

You have been a part of my life for 25+ years, holding onto every line and note in every song... knowing just how to help me emote during the dark times. Filling my drunken nights with music to feel/fill the pain... you always knew just what was needed with the pain and suffering. I looked to you as an idealized husband and then a father.

It gave me such great joy to see you sober and so happy in your family life. You inspired me to get and remain sober. I'll never forget your grin when we talked about sobriety and how the "roller coaster was gone" and life could be lived.

The week between my son's death and burial will now be changed again. I promise, though, to persevere and thrive even in my *Euphoria Mourning* because that is how you would want it to be. Say Hello to my Boy in Heaven. *Thank You*. Now you can sing this song to my Robbie just as I shared with you I had done Saturday mornings over blueberry cereal. Until we meet again.

Photo: Dawn Belotti

Tina Marie Chappell

Been a fan since MTV first played "Outshined". This is just killing me. CC was and always will be my rock god father of grunge. He helped me in so many ways in life, even with depression and when I go into my shell I put him on and I come out of my shell. Thank you, Chris for everything. Your words, music helped me out for many years. Thank you, my rock god. Love you forever. R.I.P Chris, fly with the angels and sing like you always done. Loud Love.

Tom McMahon

In stories of sweet sunshowers and black hole suns alike, Chris Cornell helped the rest of us find light through darkness, and in his songs and voice we are transported to a place where we can watch our own seasons roll on by, comforted by a soaring voice for the ages and captivated by the words of a poet after our own hearts. This man with a generous spirit and a charitable, reassuring smile inspired us with brilliant performances, sophisticated songwriting, and a work ethic and will to continue to push himself and his craft to greater and greater heights.

He will inspire generations to come with his powerful songs, incredible talent, and a career filled with unique and diverse artistry, and he will be sorely missed by those who knew him best, far away from the sights and sounds of performing stages. For these and many other reasons we will now and forever celebrate the life of Chris Cornell.

Toni Harvey

My story begins almost six years ago. One fateful evening June 22, 2011 my 13 year old son, a friend, and my son's twin sister were returning home from riding rip sticks just a mile from home. It was getting dark. A car traveling 65 mph hit my son Hayden from behind. He missed the girls only by inches. My son sustained massive head injuries and two days after the accident he lost his life. He remained on life support just long enough to become an organ donor. Needless to say "I" his mother "Fell on Black Days". As did his twin sister and his other siblings and father. It was a very surreal time in our lives.

I found some comfort in one particular song. "Say Hello to Heaven". I bet I have played it 10,000 times over the past six years. It brought me comfort during the darkest days of my life.

I began to think no one could possibly know how much pain I was in, especially if they had never lost on this level. As I began to get more into Chris's music, I also wanted to know more about the man who was singing these deep emotional songs that somehow brought me a sense of peace in a time of deep sorrow. As I researched every article about he and Andrew Wood, I began to understand the meanings behind his song "Say Hello to Heaven". He knew a part of my pain. I knew a part of his pain. He was suddenly more like me. Broken but surviving. That quality to survive the pain instead of defining yourself in the pain was what drew me to his music. He gave me hope that I would be with my son one day again. In his most beautiful vocal ability and lyrics he changed my life.

Thank you Chris Cornell. Just simply thank you.

Tony Hejnicki

Couldn't believe the news, it had to be a bad dream
He was one for those in times of trouble
Reached down, picked us all up
Impossible to imagine the future without him
Scar upon the sky

Change the past, if any of us could
Only he could sing that way
Reality starts to set in, sets in hard
Nothing more to say
Emotions ebb and flow like the tide
Listen to the words sang
Loud love to you all

Tuire Höynälä

Whole lotta love, Chris Cornell! Thank you for your music. Thank you for everything! Your music has been for years my joy, my support and my comfort when I've been so alone and depressed, in pain. Thanks for "Be(ing) Yourself", that's my mission, a way to Highway.

Tyler Ruffle McDonald

Don't want to be repetitive, but reading everyone's stories and connections with Chris and the band has really helped, so I wanted to share mine.

I want to start with acknowledging that while we are all hurting, I really feel for his wife and kids, as well as Kim, Ben and Matt. While this is hard to deal with for us, I can't even imagine what they're going through. The one thing giving me a bit of solace is that we loved Chris, and I know he knew that, and I know he loved us too.

My mom got me into Soundgarden. As much crap as I give her for her taste in music (and movies, but that's another story) she is the reason I was introduced to them. Throughout my childhood I can always remember her playing, and loving, "Spoonman". Something about the song always stuck with me, and combined with "Black Hole Sun" I really always had an understanding of who Soundgarden was.

I was 11 when *Out of Exile* came out, and something about the vocals in "Be Yourself" really did it for me. I know a lot of people here will remember, liking Audioslave was not the socially acceptable thing to do. A lot of people kind of saw them as ruining two bands to make one not as good as either predecessor. My mom, the ardent Cornell fan she was, really liked Audioslave.

But it wasn't until I was maybe 12 that everything clicked. I was in my dad's car, and had Lithium on Sirius. "The Day I Tried to Live" came on. Admittedly, the beginning of the song bored me a bit. But something about those vocals, and the combination of four seemingly simple parts coming together to make a beautifully complex piece of music that did it for me. I recognized the band name, and needed more. That day I listened to "Mind Riot". That was it. Game over. Soundgarden was my favourite band. The vocals in "Mind Riot", and the pure emotion in Cornell's voice, magic. So I was 12, and my favourite band wasn't a band. None of my friends knew who they were, and very few people cared. At 14, I decided I needed to grow my hair out. Not just long, but shoulder length. I needed to look like Chris, I needed to be Chris.

Then it happened. I know everyone reading this gets chills, and can remember where they were. January 1, 2010. Chris tweeted what seemed like a reunion. Still most were unsure, yet others promised this is what it was. Then April 16 happened, the Nudedragons show. I remember waking up the next morning scouring YouTube for every possible video of the show. I remember everything going quiet after Lollapalooza, and thinking I'd missed my opportunity to see them. Then April 2011, what seemed like the impossible happened, the tour.

I was 17, armed with my mom's credit card, and ready to make anything happen. I managed to get two pairs of fan club floor tickets, one for the first show in Toronto and one for the second two and a half hours away in London. There wasn't even a second thought about who was coming with me. The one defender of Soundgarden, fan of Chris, and influential force in my life on the matter (also the person who's credit card I charged the tickets to), my mom. I remember a five hour wait in sweltering heat outside the Molson Amphitheatre in Toronto. We were just to the left of centre stage, on the rail. I got choked up hearing the beginning of "Black Rain" as the band came out. Something amazing happened that night, and still lives on YouTube today. Before "Rusty Cage", Chris acknowledges who he refers to as "a young man" on the rail mouthing 'I love you' at him. He mentions that this shared moment with the young man is a cool 'I love you'. I can't explain why I did it, why I said it, or how it felt that he mentioned it. But my formative years were based on me loving him, and his music.

The next night in London I met Jaye and Mike English. Not only did they snap a super cool picture of my mom and I (which I sent her as soon as I heard the news about Chris, and sent her into tears), but they shared the entire experience with us. Those two shows, the five-hour waits outside both days, and seeing my favourite band, were everything. At 17, there is nothing cooler than being that close to someone you have idolized for what seems like ever. What was okay to me at the time, but is much better now was that I got to share that with my mom.

In 2012 I moved to Manchester, England for university. Of course when Soundgarden announced a quick four-stop tour with one of them in England, I made it happen. Explaining to my new friends, and roommates that I needed to make a two and a half hour train journey to London to see a band they had never heard of wasn't easy. But it was completely necessary. I got to see Soundgarden one more time, as they toured with NIN. I think the most amazing part to me was that they were great every single time. Every time felt just as amazing as the first. Every time I was left in awe. I was also lucky enough to see Chris three times on his Songbook tours. This is where I got to see the kind of person he was. Of course in a small intimate setting people were yelling song requests. Some reasonable ("Black Hole Sun"), and some downright ridiculous ("Drawing Flies"). One man yelled for "Dandelion", to which Chris responded that he needed to warm up his voice first. Sure enough, he came back around to it and played the song. Watching him fiddle around with his guitar, and work his way through songs acoustically was amazing.

Now, I don't have the personal connections with

BY THE FANS AND FRIENDS OF CHRIS CORNELL

Soundgarden music getting me through tough times like a lot of people have talked about, but it has literally been the soundtrack to my life. I think the amazing thing about Chris, and maybe the power that he had, was that he could admit he wrote a song about nothing, or had throwaway lines about nothing, yet all of those mean so many different things to all of us. When I say he will be missed, that's truly an understatement. I'm thankful that he gave us everything we loved about him, and I really, truly hope he knew how much we all loved him. It doesn't end here though, his impact will continue to be felt for quite some time. No one sings like you anymore.

Photo: Dawn Belotti.

With Soundgarden, Webster Hall, June 2, 2014.

Uo Kaolly

Thank you, Chris Cornell, you always save my life with your songs and all of your creation.

I will remember your lively performance with Soundgarden, Audioslave, Temple of The Dog, and at solo shows. You're my most favorite singer forever.

No one sings like you anymore.

Kaori xxx

THANK YOU: A TRIBUTE TO CHRIS CORNELL

Val J.

Chris, I had been struggling pretty badly with depression when I found your music. You helped me in so many ways and really inspired me to keep working on my own musical journey.

I only saw you perform live once, but it was the best thing I've ever seen. Your acoustic version of "Blow Up The Outside World" had me in awe for days.

I'll never forget that and all that you have done for me. You took a piece of me with you when you departed this world. I liked knowing that you were out there, somewhere. It helped keep me going when I was feeling down - knowing that you had dealt with so many tough times yourself and been able to overcome them.

You have done more for the world than you could possibly imagine. You will be forever missed. You are the shape of the hole inside my heart. I hope you've found peace, wherever you are.

RIP, Mr. Cornell. -Val J.

Vicky Appenzeller

I have been a fan of Chris and Soundgarden for as long as I can remember. I always wanted to see them live, but I was told I was too young for concerts. So I have posters, CDs, rares, you name it.

Since I have food allergies, I usually hate Halloween (candy). My mom found out Audioslave was coming to Camden, NJ and surprised me with tickets! I was so excited! She knew some of their songs, but at the end of the show, she was amazed of how many she knew. She laughed and said she thought they were another band. She was a fan for life (and still wears her tour shirt today!)

Then one day in 2008, I heard that Projekt Revolution was coming to Camden, NJ. I was not excited due to the fact I am not a Linkin Park fan. My ex-husband was begging me to get tickets. Eh. When I went to work the next day, they announced the full line up, which included Chris Cornell! Needless to say, I ran out to the mall to Ticketmaster to get our tickets!!

Lawn seats, sweat, and the awesomeness of fans, I was there! The act that was on before Chris (I can't remember who, sorry) had people out in the lawn with "leap frog" signs. I walked up and asked them what it meant. The guy said if I passed him my lawn ticket, he would upgrade me.

Ok, let me think.. Chris Cornell is up next... WHERE IS MY ticket!!? I traded them both (my ex and mine) in and got just inside the pavilion. I was shaking with excitement and was singing at the top of my lungs when Chris started to perform. Just about the end, Chester Bennington from LP came out to join Chris on stage. They started to play "Hunger Strike" and then I saw it... Chris was jumping off stage... and was going to walk around! oh my goodness! I jumped over seven rows of seats (empty) in front of me and stood in the walkway... shaking, crying, sweating!!! As Chris came around to where I was, he was singing and put his arm around me for a few steps!! Oh my goodness!! My heart stopped! I was shaking more than I thought I ever would! And my smile? Ear to ear!!

I got back to my seat, and my ex asked me how was it? I was making no sense... just shrieking and smiling! He was worried, so he called my mom. He said I don't know if she's ok, or what's going on. My mom asked me what happened and I was still a mess not making any sense! She laughed! She knew I was fine!!

As much as I wanted to see and experience Chris' music in person, nothing will top his persona! The range in his singing, the lyrics and his contributions to music is phenomenal. Who would have thought a rock genius would ask Timbaland to do a record? That was one of the things that I think made Chris so well loved! He didn't just put all the eggs in one basket, he had no boundaries to his creativity.

I wish we knew what else he had in mind months, years from now. The songs will live on forever with me for sure (helping me through many years of depression and anxiety myself). I just wish we didn't have to write these words down for him.

Vincent Meeks

Chris Cornell was always like the friend I never actually had, knew exactly what I was thinking, and sang and wrote songs like I always wanted to write and sing. His music just reached out like no other music could and will always be a part of my DNA.

Vincent.

Wonder Sar

In Canberra 2011 you made me laugh. You suggested they might sell fluffy toys that look like you. They'd smell like peppermint and when you squeeze them a little bit of sweat comes out.

In Canberra 2015 you saw an advert at the venue for a woman who claimed she could speak to the spirits of the dead. Between songs you pondered this multiple times, you were sceptical. Towards the end, you questioned, what if it's true? What if there are spirits all around me thinking 'who is this dickhead?' We laughed. Now you know the answer, and I'm wondering who that woman was.

Yvonne Photias

A big collective hug going out to all of Chris' fans, whom I'm sure are as affected by his sudden and unexpected passing as I am. To put it mildly, I am devastated. I will be forever heartbroken and shattered by the news I received from my nephew via text message at 6am (California time) on May 18th. After that text there was another, then another, then another, from friends and family. And everyone said the same thing... "you were the first person I thought of."

Chris was front and center in my life for the better part of 30 years, and everyone knew it. He had the power to affect people. He didn't have to try. He reached in and took hold of your heart and soul. His voice, his presence... was like a magnet. It was a constant combination of incredible opposites that melted together to become beautifully... him. Extreme vulnerability, powerful strength, in lyric and voice. And oh, that voice. I could write a book on every nuance of tone, melody and lyrical content.

I had the privilege of seeing Chris live at three of the Songbook Tours... May 2011 at Humphrey by the Bay on Shelter Island (San Diego), then again in December 2011 at the Orpheum Theater in Los Angeles, and October 2013 at the Balboa theater in San Diego. The first show at Humphreys sold out so quickly I went to eBay and got one ticket. I drove alone from just outside of Palm Springs. I think I was in the 27th row. There was a sweet usher who kept checking on me... I kept telling her I was fine... more than fine. Sooo excited I could barely contain myself. About five minutes before the show started, she came and got me... "would you like to sit in the third row?" I WAS OUT OF MY SEAT BEFORE SHE FINISHED THE SENTENCE! I sat in the third row next to a really sweet couple. They were as into it as me. We had such a great time, sang along to every song. Toward the end we all stood right in front of the stage for the last couple of songs. Chris was in the middle of a breathtaking version of "Imagine" and there were two young girls standing in front of me backs to stage, loudly talking making plans for after the show. I entered their conversation with "you guys! ... turn around... LISTEN!... you are in the presence of GREATNESS!!"

When Temple of the Dog reunited I was ecstatic to witness the magic at the Los Angeles Forum in November 2016. By no coincidence (in my mind and heart,) Temple of the Dog was released on the exact day I was discharged from Northridge Hospital after an almost three month stay, April 26, 1991. It was all I listened to for the following six months as I adjusted to life as an amputee. The album literally saved me. Chris' voice resonating within me saved me from drowning in self pity. I had a place to channel my emotions...

If anything, I just wish I could have simply told him thank you. You made a difference. I never had the chance to meet Chris in person, but we did make eye contact once and he smiled. That was enough for me. He knew I was there. Thank you Chris for sharing your voice, your charm, your talent and your essence with this world. We are all blessed to have been a part of you. Wherever your journey has taken you now, I wish you all the peace and love that you deserve.

With love and thanks,
Yvonne (Photias) Ochoa La Quinta, California.

BY THE FANS AND FRIENDS OF CHRIS CORNELL

(For another photo, see page 57)

Zacarius Hill

I would like to say that I've never met the man, unfortunately. However, I've never been so positively influenced by a person I've never met (other than God). This dude had such deep meaning in every one of his songs. You could tell he really meant every. Single. Word. He. Sang. A lot of people told me his songs were "depressing" but it couldn't be anything further from the truth. "Like a Stone" was a little slow, yeah, but by far one of his most popular songs. Then you look at "Be Yourself"...

I am far from musically talented... but I've been through some shit in my life that's made me (on more than one occasion) sit in my car and just belt that song out at the top of my lungs. Had me "screaming at the top of my head" so to speak. His voice was so different and so great I could pick it out from anything. Casino Royale's intro... MTV when they played his song "Scream" a few times just because it was Chris Cornell singing. Anyone else wouldn't have taken that song as far up the charts as it went.

But ultimately, even after his untimely death. I sit here like a like a stone. And think back to many of his songs darker deeper meanings. Anything from his earlier "Pretty Noose" or "The Day I Tried to Live" to his more recent "Nearly Forgot my Broken Heart" and can't help but think his whole life (for the most part) was a cry for help. He struggled with many things like drug addiction to bi-polar mood disorder (I've heard). And nothing has motivated me more to be a better person in my life to anyone I meet. Because you really don't know what someone is going through at any point in time.

So he. Chris Cornell. A man I've never met and never will. Has had a bigger impact on me than anyone else. More than people I actually do know. And I feel like that positivity he showed every now and then in his lyrics has shown me why it's so crucial. And I didn't find out until after his passing that he was an avid Obama supporter. In a time where people kill because someone has differing views on politics. I couldn't have more love for Chris even though we saw politics very differently.

"Say Hello to Heaven" for me Chris. You will be deeply, deeply missed... because I've lost a friend I've never got the chance to meet.

THANK YOU: A TRIBUTE TO CHRIS CORNELL

Photo: Dawn Belotti.

With Soundgarden, Webster Hall, June 2, 2014.

Zær Ben Abdallah

I just wrote a song about us as fans for Chris Cornell.

Voice of Our Generation

Verse 1:

Mourning since the 17th, knowing that you 're gone
Bleeding heart is aching, my childhood just passed out
Drowning in a sea of sorrow, my sun won't shine tomorrow
Believing I was all alone until I found my home

Pre-chorus:

Millions candles in the dark shiny sky
Paying a tribute to our hero the dark knight

THANK YOU: A TRIBUTE TO CHRIS CORNELL

Chorus:

You're the voice of our generation
That travels through the skies
You're the voice of our generation
An artist of all time

Verse 2:

The demons who just took you thought, we were going to forget you
Nothing seems to kill you brother, no matter how they tried.

Chorus:

You're the voice of our generation
That travels through the skies
You're the voice of our generation
An artist of all time

Final Words

Thank You has been a labour of love. This paperback edition has been priced at the minimum amount possible, to cover production and distribution costs. A free ebook version is also available. Making money was never the intention in creating this book.

I have immense gratitude to all the contributors to the book. This simply wouldn't exist without you. I hope I have done your expectations justice.

I am also overwhelmed with the amazing support this project has been given. An idea I had for a little project to help process my own grief has blossomed into something so much more.

Thank you for letting me do this.

This is our book. YOUR book.

Angela J. Maher
(Editor)

Manufactured by Amazon.ca
Bolton, ON